off the grill... and on the rug
great outdoor eats

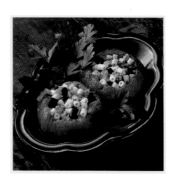

off the grill... and on the rug
great outdoor eats

the complete barbecue and picnic recipe collection

emma summer

southwater

This edition is published by Southwater

Distributed in the UK by
The Manning Partnership
251–253 London Road East
Batheaston
Bath BAI 7RL
tel. 01225 852 727
fax 01225 852 852

Published in the USA by
Anness Publishing Inc.
27 West 20th Street
Suite 504
New York
NY 10011
fax 212 807 6813

Distributed in Canada by
General Publishing
895 Don Mills Road
400–402 Park Centre
Toronto, Ontario M3C IW3
tel. 416 445 3333
fax 416 445 5991

Distributed in Australia by
Sandstone Publishing
Unit I, 360 Norton Street
Leichhardt
New South Wales 2040
tel. 02 9560 7888
fax 02 9560 7488

Southwater is an imprint of Anness Publishing Limited
Hermes House, 88–89 Blackfriars Road, London SEI 8HA
tel. 020 7401 2077; fax 020 7633 9499

© Anness Publishing Limited 1999, 2002

Publisher Joanna Lorenz
Project Editor Sarah Ainley
Editor Emma Gray
Copy Editor Jenni Fleetwood
Designers Patrick McLeavey & Jo Brewer
Illustrator Anna Koska
Photographers Edward Allwright, James Duncan, Michelle Garrett,
Amanda Heywood, Tim Hill, Don Last & Debbie Patterson
Editorial Reader Joy Wotton
Recipes Carla Capalbo, Jacqueline Clark, Carole Clements, Matthew Drennan, Joanna Farrow, Christine France,
Carole Handslip, Sarah Maxwell, Angela Nilson, Liz Trigg, Steven Wheeler & Elizabeth Wolf-Cohen
Previously published as *Barbecues & Picnics*

1 3 5 7 9 10 8 6 4 2

NOTES
For all recipes, quantities are given in both metric and imperial measures and, where appropriate,
measures are also given in standard cups and spoons. Follow one set, but not a mixture, because
they are not interchangeable.
Standard spoon and cup measures are level.
I tsp = 5ml, I tbsp = 15ml, I cup = 250ml/8fl oz
Australian standard tablespoons are 20ml. Australian readers should use
3 tsp in place of I tbsp for measuring small quantities of gelatine, flour, salt, etc.
Medium eggs are used unless otherwise stated.

Contents

Part One: Perfect Barbecues

Introduction 8

Meats 14

Poultry 26

Fish & Seafood 36

Vegetables &

Vegetarian Dishes 46

Desserts 56

Part Two: Perfect Picnics

Introduction 68

Finger Food 74

Salad Days 86

Main Attractions 98

Sweet Treats 112

Index 127

Perfect Barbecues

There is nothing more evocative of warm summer days enjoyed with family and friends than the delectable aromas of a barbecue. Here is the perfect combination of mouthwatering recipes that will have everyone eager to help with the cooking.

Introduction

There can be no finer stimulus to the appetite than the sight and aroma of good food grilling on the barbecue, and no more relaxing way to entertain family and friends.

As with so many aspects of cookery, success depends as much upon forethought as it does on flair. It is no use getting all fired up, only to find there's not enough fuel, or that you haven't bought any buns for the burgers. Good equipment is easy to acquire, enthusiasm is a ready commodity, but expertise is largely a matter of planning and practice.

What type of barbecue should you choose? The range is vast, from small disposable foil containers to state-of-the-art gas or electric cooking stations. If you are new to this style of cooking, start with a

basic brazier or kettle. The former is simply a firebox on legs, with vents or dampers to control the air flow to the burning coals, and a grill with a variable height. A kettle is a bowl-shaped barbecue with a domed hood that reflects the heat and speeds up the cooking process, and can also act as a shield if rain threatens to blight your fire.

Both braziers and kettles usually have wheels, plus one or two solid legs for anchorage. The advantage of this is that you can move the barbecue if the wind changes direction, a point to consider if you plan to build an outdoor cooking and eating area. Make sure the site is sheltered, handy for the house and away from vegetation. Locate the fire so that the prevailing wind blows smoke away from the area.

The most efficient way to build a solid-fuel fire is to spread a 5cm/2in deep layer of wood, lump charcoal or briquettes on the grate, with more fuel piled up in a pyramid in the centre. Push one or two firelighters into the pyramid, light with a long match and leave to burn for 15 minutes before spreading out the coals. Don't start to cook until the coals are ash grey. This will take 30–45 minutes. (If you are using self-igniting briquettes, follow the manufacturer's instructions.)

Before starting to cook, make sure you have everything you need, including oven mitts, a sturdy flame-proof apron and a water-filled spray bottle for emergencies. Cooking time and temperature will vary according to the type and density of the food. Control the heat by raising or lowering the grill, or by bunching or spreading the coals. This is relatively easy when you are grilling a single item, such as a whole salmon, but cooking several different sorts of food simultaneously is more tricky: create a hot spot for steaks, sausages and cutlets by pushing some of the coals together in the centre, then place vegetables, delicate poultry and seafood around the rim, where the heat is less fierce. Desserts like baked bananas and glazed pineapple cook well on the dying embers.

Never be tempted to rush a barbecue. The enjoyment comes from the combination of great-tasting food and a relaxing setting, so take it slowly, steadily and safely and have some fun!

9

Barbecue Favourites

BEEF

Use high heat for beef, cutting off excess fat to minimize flare-ups. Grill 2.5cm/1in steaks for 5 minutes if you like them rare; 8 minutes for medium and 12 minutes for well done. Burgers must always be fully cooked. Test by piercing the flesh: the juices should run clear and the flesh should not have any trace of pinkness.

CHICKEN

Always a popular choice, especially when marinated. Use low heat for breasts; medium for wings, drumsticks or quarters. Allow about 15 minutes for breasts and wings; 30 minutes for other cuts and poussins. Chicken must be thoroughly cooked; it is a good idea to pre-cook chicken in the microwave or oven and then transfer it straight to the barbecue. Chicken should not be reheated once it has cooled.

FISH

Keep the heat low to medium. Slash whole fish to conduct the heat to the bone. Cook firm-fleshed varieties on the grill, but wrap delicate fish in foil, with lemon and butter. Oily fish bastes itself. Finish it off over high heat to crisp the skin. Allow about 10 minutes per 2.5cm/1in thickness for whole fish over 2.25kg/5lb; as for smaller whole fish, steaks and cutlets, the fish is ready when the flesh flakes easily when tested with a sharp knife.

FRUIT

Bananas are brilliant; just place them on the grill and they'll cook in their skins to tender perfection. Try pineapple and apples in foil, too.

LAMB

Cook leg steaks and chops over medium heat for 10–15 minutes; kebabs can take less time. A butterflied leg of lamb cooks very successfully in about an hour.

PORK

Fillet is great for kebabs. Cubes or chops about 2.5cm/1in thick need about 15 minutes over medium heat. Spare ribs take 30–40 minutes, while thick sausages should be cooked in 15–20 minutes. All pork must be thoroughly cooked; start sausages off in the microwave if you like.

SHELLFISH

Peeled prawns and scallops are delicate, so keep the heat low and baste them often. Shell-on crustaceans can take moderate heat and will need slightly longer (as a rough guide, give large prawns in the shell 6–8 minutes; peeled prawns 4–6 minutes). Cook mussels until they open.

VEGETABLES

Wrap potatoes and squash in foil and cook them in the coals; cook mushrooms with herb butter in foil on the grill. Grilled aubergines, tomatoes, onions, peppers and courgettes taste superb. For timings, see individual recipes.

NOTE: All cooking times are approximate.

SAFETY TIPS

Make sure the barbecue stands on level ground.
Never leave a fire unattended.
Keep children and animals away.
Never pour flammable liquid on to the barbecue.
Wear a flameproof apron and use mitts and long-handled tools.
Smother the fire after cooking.

Techniques

COOKING IN FOIL

Delicate foods, or foods that are best cooked in their own juices, can be cooked in foil either on the grill rack or directly in the coals of the fire with more robust items, like potatoes and squash. Cut two equal pieces of heavy-duty foil, to make a double layer for extra strength, large enough to wrap the food. Lightly grease the foil with melted butter or oil, then place the food in the centre of the foil and add any flavourings or seasonings. Wrap parcels securely, twisting the edges of the foil together, so that the juices cannot escape during cooking.

PREPARING WHOLE FISH

Small oily fish, such as mackerel or trout, cook perfectly on the barbecue. Unless the fishmonger has already done so, cut off the fins and strip out the gills with kitchen scissors. Hold the fish firmly at the tail end and use the back of a small knife blade to remove the scales, scraping towards the head end. Rinse well in cold water, then slit the fish from under the tail to behind the gills to open up the belly. Remove and discard the entrails and rinse the cavity thoroughly. Rub the cavity with salt and rinse again. Dry with kitchen paper.

12

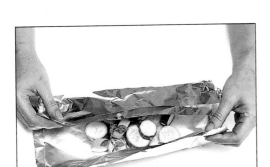

Marinating

Marinades add flavour and moisture and are also used to tenderize foods, especially meat. Oil is usually included in a savoury marinade, the amount governed by whether the food is lean or has a relatively high fat content. Arrange the food in a single layer, pour over the marinade and turn the food to coat it evenly.

Cover and chill for the recommended time, turning occasionally. When cooking, baste with the remaining marinade, but be careful if it is high in oil or alcohol, as flare-ups can occur. Sweet bastes containing sugar or honey burn readily; brush them over the food towards the end of the cooking time.

Basic Marinade (for meat or fish)
Mix 1 crushed garlic clove with 45ml/3 tbsp each of sunflower oil and dry sherry. Stir in 15ml/1 tbsp each of Worcestershire sauce and dark soy sauce. Add a grinding of black pepper.

Herb Marinade (for fish or chicken)
Mix 120ml/4fl oz/½ cup dry white wine with 60ml/4 tbsp olive oil and 15ml/1 tbsp lemon juice. Add 30ml/2 tbsp finely chopped fresh herbs and a grinding of black pepper.

Citrus Marinade (for duck or pork)
Mix 5ml/1 tsp each of grated lemon, lime and orange rind with 30ml/2 tbsp each of lemon, lime and orange juice. Add 45ml/3 tbsp sunflower oil, 30ml/2 tbsp clear honey and 15ml/1 tbsp soy sauce. Whisk in 5ml/1 tsp Dijon mustard.

Red Wine Marinade (for beef or game)
Mix 150ml/¼ pint/⅔ cup dry red wine with 15ml/1 tbsp each of olive oil and red wine vinegar, 3 crushed garlic cloves and 2 crumbled bay leaves.

13

Meats

Five-spice Ribs

INGREDIENTS

1kg/2¼lb Chinese-style pork spare ribs
2.5ml/½ tsp sweet chilli sauce
60ml/4 tbsp soy sauce
15ml/1 tbsp sunflower oil
10ml/2 tsp Chinese five-spice powder
2 garlic cloves, crushed
15ml/1 tbsp grated fresh root ginger
45ml/3 tbsp dark muscovado sugar
4 spring onions, to serve

SERVES 4

1 If the spare ribs are still joined together, either ask the butcher to separate them, or do this yourself with a sharp knife. Place the spare ribs in a large mixing bowl.

2 Mix the chilli sauce, soy sauce and oil in a separate bowl. Stir in the five-spice powder, garlic, ginger and sugar. Mix well, then pour the mixture over the ribs. Turn the ribs to coat them thoroughly. Cover the bowl and marinate overnight in the fridge.

3 Cook the ribs on a moderately hot barbecue, turning frequently, for 30–40 minutes. Brush occasionally with the remaining marinade.

4 Slice the spring onions. Serve the cooked spare ribs on a platter, with the spring onions scattered over the top.

COOK'S TIP
Make sure you buy authentic Chinese five-spice powder and not five-spice seasoning, which is much saltier.

Tex-Mex Burgers

INGREDIENTS

500g / 1¼lb / 2½ cups lean minced beef
1 small onion, finely chopped
1 small green pepper, seeded and finely chopped
1 garlic clove, crushed
oil, for brushing
4 fresh tortillas
salt and ground black pepper
chopped fresh coriander, to garnish
lettuce, to serve (optional)
GUACAMOLE
2 ripe avocados, halved and stoned
1 garlic clove, crushed
2 tomatoes, chopped
juice of 1 lime or lemon
½ small fresh green chilli, seeded and chopped
30ml / 2 tbsp chopped fresh coriander

SERVES 4

1 Combine the minced beef with the onion, pepper and garlic in a bowl. Add plenty of salt and pepper. Mix well, then divide the mixture into four portions.

2 Carefully shape each portion into a round burger, using dampened hands or a burger press. Cover with a cloth and set aside while you make the guacamole.

3 Scoop the avocado flesh into a bowl and mash roughly with a fork, then mix in the garlic, tomatoes, lime or lemon juice, chilli and coriander. Add salt and pepper to taste. Cover the surface of the guacamole closely with clear film.

4 Brush the burgers lightly with oil. Grill on a moderately hot barbecue for 8–10 minutes or until cooked through. Turn the burgers once during cooking.

5 Just before serving, heat the tortillas on the barbecue for about 15 seconds on each side. Add a spoonful of guacamole and a burger to each tortilla, then fold the tortilla over. Garnish with chopped coriander and serve plain or with lettuce.

Peppered Steak in Beer & Garlic

INGREDIENTS

4 beef sirloin or rump steaks, 2.5cm/1in thick,
about 175g/6oz each
2 garlic cloves, crushed
120ml/4fl oz/½ cup brown ale or stout
30ml/2 tbsp dark muscovado sugar
30ml/2 tbsp Worcestershire sauce
15ml/1 tbsp corn oil
15ml/1 tbsp crushed black peppercorns

SERVES 4

1 Place the steaks in a single layer in a shallow dish. Mix the garlic, ale or stout, sugar, Worcestershire sauce and oil in a jug. Pour the mixture over the meat, turn to coat evenly, then cover and marinate in the fridge for 2–3 hours or overnight.

2 Lift the steaks out of the dish. Reserve the marinade. Sprinkle the peppercorns evenly over the steaks and press them into the surface.

3 Cook the steaks on a hot barbecue for 3–6 minutes on each side or until done to your taste. Turn them once during cooking and use the reserved marinade for basting. Serve each steak with a baked potato and a mixed salad, if you like.

COOK'S TIP
Use the marinade sparingly as the alcohol
will cause flare-ups if so much is used that
it drips on to the coals. Brush on a small
amount at a time.

Racks of Lamb with Lavender Marinade

INGREDIENTS

4 racks of lamb, each with 3–4 cutlets
1 shallot, finely chopped
45ml / 3 tbsp chopped fresh lavender
15ml / 1 tbsp balsamic vinegar
30ml / 2 tbsp olive oil
15ml / 1 tbsp lemon juice
salt and ground black pepper
handful of lavender sprigs

SERVES 4

1 Place the racks of lamb in a large bowl or wide dish and sprinkle the chopped shallot over the top. Crumble the lavender between your fingers to release

the scent and distribute it over the lamb.

2 Mix the vinegar, oil and lemon juice in a small bowl. Whisk with a fork, then pour over the lamb. Sprinkle with salt and pepper to taste, and turn to coat evenly.

3 Scatter a few lavender sprigs over the grill or on the coals of a moderately hot barbecue. Lift the lamb out of the marinade and place it on the barbecue grill. Cook for 15–20 minutes or until golden brown on the outside and slightly pink in the centre. Baste occasionally with the remaining marinade. Serve the lamb hot, garnished with more lavender sprigs.

VARIATION

Use rosemary sprigs instead of lavender, if you prefer. They give off a wonderful aroma when burned on the barbecue.

19

Bacon Kofta Kebabs with Bulgur Salad

INGREDIENTS

250g/9oz lean streaky bacon rashers, chopped
1 small onion, chopped
1 celery stick, chopped
75ml/5 tbsp fresh wholemeal breadcrumbs
45ml/3 tbsp chopped fresh thyme
30ml/2 tbsp Worcestershire sauce
beaten egg, to bind
salt and ground black pepper
oil, for brushing
BULGUR SALAD
115g/4oz/⅔ cup bulgur wheat
60ml/4 tbsp toasted sunflower seeds
30ml/2 tbsp olive oil
handful of celery leaves, chopped

SERVES 4

1 Soak 8 bamboo skewers in cold water for 30 minutes. Place the bacon, onion, celery and bread-crumbs in a food processor. Process until finely chopped. Add the thyme and Worcestershire sauce, with salt and pepper to taste. Process briefly. With the motor running, add just enough beaten egg to bind the mixture.

2 Using a knife, scrape the bacon mixture on to a board, then with dampened hands, divide the mixture into eight equal portions. Drain the bamboo skew-ers and shape each portion of bacon mixture into a long sausage, moulding and pressing it on to a skewer. Chill the kofta kebabs in the fridge while you make the bulgur salad.

3 Place the bulgur wheat in a large bowl. Pour over boiling water to cover. Leave to stand for 30 minutes or until the grains are tender, then tip into a sieve lined with muslin or a clean dish towel. Drain well, then gather up the sides of the cloth and squeeze out as much liquid as possible from the bulgur. Tip it into a serving bowl.

4 Add the sunflower seeds and oil to the bowl, with salt and ground black pepper to taste. Stir in the chopped celery leaves and set the salad aside.

5 Cook the kofta kebabs over a moderately hot barbecue for 8–10 minutes, brushing with oil and turning occasionally to ensure that they are cooked through. Leaving the kofta kebabs on the bamboo skewers, serve with the bulgur salad.

Mixed Grill Skewers with Horseradish Butter

INGREDIENTS

4 small lamb noisettes, about 2.5cm/1in thick
4 lamb's kidneys
8 rindless streaky bacon rashers
8 cherry tomatoes
8 chipolata sausages
20 bay leaves
HORSERADISH BUTTER
40g/1½oz/3 tbsp butter
30ml/2 tbsp horseradish relish
salt and ground black pepper

SERVES 4

22

1 Trim any excess fat from the lamb noisettes. Cut the kidneys in half and remove the cores with scissors. Cut each bacon rasher in half widthways, then wrap each piece around a tomato or a half-kidney.

2 Carefully thread the lamb noisettes, chipolatas, bay leaves and wrapped tomatoes and kidneys on to four long metal skewers. Spear the meat through the side to present the largest possible area to the heat.

3 Melt the butter in a small pan. Stir in the horseradish relish. Brush a little of the mixture over the skewered meats and sprinkle with salt and pepper.

4 Grill the skewers on a moderately hot barbecue for 12–15 minutes, turning occasionally until all the ingredients are cooked through. Keep the rest of the horseradish butter warm by standing the pan on the edge of the barbecue grill. Pour it over the skewers to serve.

VARIATION
Use chunks of pork fillet instead of kidneys, if you prefer. Mushrooms and baby onions would make a good addition.

Char-grilled Sausages with Prunes & Bacon

INGREDIENTS

8 large, meaty pork sausages
30ml/2 tbsp Dijon mustard
24 ready-to-eat prunes
8 rindless smoked streaky bacon rashers

SERVES 4

1 With a sharp knife, make a long slit in one side of each sausage, cutting about three-quarters of the way through, so that each sausage can be opened out to make a long, narrow pocket.

2 Spread the cut surface of each pocket with mustard, then place three prunes in the middle of each sausage, pressing them down firmly to secure.

3 Using the back of a knife, stretch the bacon rashers out thinly, then wrap a rasher around each filled sausage to hold it in shape. Use cocktail sticks (soaked in water to prevent scorching) to secure the bacon, if necessary.

4 Grill the wrapped sausages over a hot barbecue for 15–18 minutes, turning occasionally, until evenly browned and cooked through.

COOK'S TIP
Specialist butchers pride themselves on selling a wide variety of flavoured sausages. Vary this recipe with venison sausages, or try pork sausages with apple.

Pork & Pineapple Satay

INGREDIENTS

500g / 1¼lb pork fillet
1 small onion, chopped
1 garlic clove, chopped
60ml / 4 tbsp soy sauce
finely grated rind of ½ lemon
5ml / 1 tsp ground cumin
5ml / 1 tsp ground coriander
5ml / 1 tsp ground turmeric
5ml / 1 tsp dark muscovado sugar
225g / 8oz can pineapple chunks, drained
SATAY SAUCE
175ml / 6fl oz / ¾ cup coconut milk
115g / 4oz / 6 tbsp crunchy peanut butter
1 garlic clove, crushed
10ml / 2 tsp soy sauce
5ml / 1 tsp dark muscovado sugar

SERVES 4

1 Soak 4 long or 8 short bamboo skewers in water for 30 minutes. Trim any fat from the pork fillet and cut it into 2.5cm/1in cubes. Place the meat in a large bowl.

2 Combine the onion, garlic, soy sauce, lemon rind, spices and sugar in a food processor. Add 2 pineapple chunks and then process the mixture to a fairly

smooth paste. Scrape the paste into the bowl containing the pork. Toss to coat evenly.

3 Make the sauce. Pour the coconut milk into a small saucepan. Stir in the peanut butter, then add the garlic, soy sauce and sugar. Heat gently, and stir until

smooth and hot. Cover the pan and keep hot on the edge of the barbecue.

4 Drain the skewers and thread them alternately with pieces of pork and pineapple. Grill on a moderately hot barbecue for 10–12 minutes, turning occasionally, until the pork is cooked through. Serve at once, with the satay sauce.

24

Poultry

Chicken & Citrus Kebabs

INGREDIENTS

4 skinless, boneless chicken breasts
fresh mint sprigs and 4 twists each of
lime and lemon, to garnish
MARINADE
finely grated rind and juice of ½ orange
finely grated rind and juice of
½ small lemon or lime
30ml/2 tbsp olive oil
30ml/2 tbsp clear honey
30ml/2 tbsp chopped fresh mint
1.25ml/¼ tsp ground cumin
salt and ground black pepper

SERVES 4

2 Lift the chicken cubes out of the marinade and thread on to metal skewers. Grill on a moderately hot barbecue for 15 minutes, basting occasionally with the marinade. Turn the skewers frequently.

1 Cut the chicken into 2.5cm/1in cubes. To make the marinade, mix the grated citrus rind and juice in a bowl. Stir in the olive oil, honey, mint and cumin, then add

the chicken cubes and stir to coat. Cover and marinate for at least 2 hours.

3 Garnish the kebabs with mint sprigs and citrus twists. Serve with a side salad, if you like.

COOK'S TIP
Chicken breasts are tender, and will dry out over an intense fire. Cook them on the edge of the barbecue or wait until the coals are cooler.

Deep South Salad

INGREDIENTS

4 corn cobs
4 skinless, boneless chicken breasts
15ml / 1 tbsp corn oil
225g / 8oz rindless unsmoked streaky
bacon rashers
40g / 1½oz / 3 tbsp butter, softened
4 ripe bananas
4 firm tomatoes, halved
1 escarole or butterhead lettuce,
separated into leaves
1 bunch watercress, trimmed
ground black pepper
DRESSING
75ml / 5 tbsp groundnut oil
15ml / 1 tbsp white wine vinegar
10ml / 2 tsp maple syrup
10ml / 2 tsp mild mustard
15ml / 1 tbsp water

SERVES 4

1 Make the dressing by whisking all the ingredients in a bowl. Set aside. Peel back the corn husks, remove the silky threads, then fold the husks back over the kernels. Par-cook the cobs in a large saucepan of lightly salted water for about 15 minutes, until the kernels are just tender.

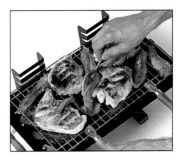

2 Meanwhile, brush the chicken breasts with oil, season them lightly with ground black pepper and grill on a low to moderately hot barbecue for 15 minutes or until cooked through, turning once. Barbecue the bacon for 8–10 minutes, until crisp.

3 Drain the corn cobs, brush the kernels with butter and barbecue, along with the whole peeled bananas and tomatoes, until lightly browned.

4 Whisk the dressing again and add the salad leaves. Toss lightly and arrange them on four large plates. Slice the hot chicken breasts and arrange them on the salad leaves, with the bacon, bananas, tomatoes and grilled corn.

28

Blackened Cajun Chicken & Corn

INGREDIENTS

8 chicken pieces
2 whole corn cobs
10ml/2 tsp garlic salt
10ml/2 tsp ground black pepper
7.5ml/1½ tsp ground cumin
7.5ml/1½ tsp paprika
5ml/1 tsp cayenne pepper
40g/1½oz/3 tbsp butter, melted
chopped parsley, to garnish

SERVES 4

1 Cut any excess fat from the chicken, but leave the skin on. Make several deep slashes in the fleshiest parts, to allow the flavours to penetrate.

2 Pull off the corn husks and remove the silky threads, then cut each cob into thick slices.

3 Mix the seasonings and spices in a small bowl. Brush the chicken and corn with melted butter and sprinkle the spices over them. Toss well to coat evenly.

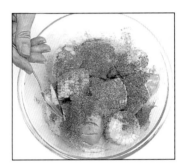

4 Grill the chicken pieces on a moderately hot barbecue for 10 minutes, turning occasionally. Add the corn and grill for a further 15 minutes, until the chicken has begun to blacken, and the corn cobs are lightly charred. Garnish with parsley and serve.

COOK'S TIP

Chicken wings cook more quickly than other joints; if you use them, grill them alongside the corn, for the same amount of time.

30

Barbecued Turkey Rolls with Gazpacho Sauce

INGREDIENTS

4 turkey breast steaks
15ml/1 tbsp red pesto
4 chorizo sausages
salt and ground black pepper
GAZPACHO SAUCE
1 green pepper, seeded and chopped
1 red pepper, seeded and chopped
7.5cm/3in piece of cucumber, roughly chopped
1 tomato, roughly chopped
1 garlic clove, roughly chopped
15ml/1 tbsp red wine vinegar
45ml/3 tbsp olive oil

SERVES 4

1 Make the sauce. Combine the peppers, cucumber, tomato and garlic in a food processor. Add the vinegar, with 30ml/2 tbsp of the oil. Process until almost smooth. Scrape into a bowl, season with salt and pepper and set aside.

2 If the turkey breasts are quite thick, place them between two sheets of clear film and flatten them slightly by pressing them firmly with a rolling pin.

3 Spread the pesto over each flattened turkey breast, add a chorizo and roll up firmly. Slice the rolls thickly, then spear them on to 4 long metal skewers. The turkey rolls should be speared though the side so that they present the largest possible area to the heat.

4 Grill on a moderately hot barbecue for 10–12 minutes, turning once. Serve at once, with the gazpacho sauce.

Sweet & Sour Kebabs

INGREDIENTS

2 skinless, boneless chicken breasts
8 baby onions
4 rindless streaky bacon rashers
2 large, firm bananas
1 red pepper, seeded and cut
into 2.5cm/1in squares
MARINADE
30ml/2 tbsp soft light brown sugar
15ml/1 tbsp Worcestershire sauce
30ml/2 tbsp lemon juice
salt and ground black pepper
HARLEQUIN RICE
30ml/2 tbsp olive oil
450g/1lb/4 cups cooked rice (about
225g/8oz/generous 1 cup raw weight)
115g/4oz/1 cup cooked peas
1 small red pepper, seeded and diced

SERVES 4

1 Make the marinade by mixing all the ingredients in a bowl. Cut each chicken breast into four pieces and add to the marinade. Toss to coat, then cover and marinate in the fridge for at least 4 hours, preferably overnight.

2 Bring a small saucepan of water to the boil. Add the onions to the pan and blanch for 5 minutes. Drain and set aside. Cut each bacon rasher in half widthways. Peel the bananas and cut each one into four pieces. Wrap a piece of bacon around each chunk of banana.

3 Lift the chicken pieces out of the marinade and then thread them on to long metal skewers, with the baby onions, bacon-wrapped banana chunks and pepper squares. Brush the kebabs with the marinade.

4 Grill on a low to moderately hot barbecue for 15 minutes, turning frequently and basting the kebabs with the marinade. Move to the edge of the barbecue to keep warm while you prepare the rice.

5 Heat the oil in a pan. Add the rice, peas and pepper and heat through. Serve with the kebabs.

Spiced Chicken Breasts with Coconut Sauce

INGREDIENTS

200g / 7oz block creamed coconut, cubed
300ml / ½ pint / 1¼ cups boiling water
3 garlic cloves, chopped
2 spring onions, chopped
1 fresh green chilli, chopped
45ml / 3 tbsp grated fresh root ginger
5ml / 1 tsp fennel seeds
2.5ml / ½ tsp black peppercorns
seeds from 4 green cardamom pods
30ml / 2 tbsp ground coriander
5ml / 1 tsp ground cumin
5ml / 1 tsp grated nutmeg
2.5ml / ½ tsp ground cloves
2.5ml / ½ tsp ground turmeric
4 large skinless, boneless chicken breasts
onion rings and fresh coriander
sprigs, to garnish

SERVES 4

1 Dissolve the coconut in the boiling water in a heatproof jug. Combine the garlic, spring onions, chilli, ginger and all the spices in a food processor or blender. Add the coconut mixture and process to a smooth paste.

2 Slash the chicken breasts in several places. Arrange them in a single layer in a shallow dish. Spoon over half the coconut mixture and toss to coat evenly. Cover and marinate for 30 minutes at room temperature, or overnight in the fridge.

3 Heat the remaining coconut mixture gently in a pan, stirring all the time, then keep it warm at the edge of the barbecue. Drain the chicken breasts and grill them over low to medium heat for 12–15 minutes, turning once, until fully cooked. Garnish with onion rings and fresh coriander sprigs. Serve with the coconut sauce.

Chicken with Herb & Ricotta Stuffing

INGREDIENTS

60ml/4 tbsp ricotta cheese
1 garlic clove, crushed
45ml/3 tbsp mixed chopped
fresh herbs (chives, flat leaf parsley
and mint)
30ml/2 tbsp fresh brown breadcrumbs
8 chicken drumsticks
8 rashers smoked streaky bacon
5ml/1 tsp wholegrain mustard
15ml/1 tbsp sunflower oil
salt and freshly ground black pepper
lettuce, to serve (optional)

SERVES 4

35

1 Make the stuffing. Mix the ricotta cheese with the garlic, herbs and breadcrumbs in a bowl. Season the mixture well with plenty of salt and black pepper.

2 Carefully loosen the skin from each drumstick and spoon a little of the herb stuffing under each, smoothing the skin back over firmly.

3 Wrap a bacon rasher around the wide end of each drumstick, to secure the skin over the stuffing.

4 Mix the mustard and oil in a bowl and brush over the chicken. Cook on a moderately hot barbecue for 20–25 minutes, turning occasionally, until the chicken is cooked through. Serve with lettuce, if you like.

Fish & Seafood

Char-grilled Tuna with Fiery Pepper Purée

INGREDIENTS

4 tuna steaks, about 175g/6oz each
finely grated rind and juice of 1 lime
30ml/2 tbsp olive oil
salt and ground black pepper
lime wedges, to serve
PEPPER PURÉE
2 red peppers, seeded and halved
1 small onion
2 garlic cloves, crushed
2 fresh red chillies, sliced
1 slice of white bread without crusts, diced
45ml/3 tbsp olive oil, plus extra for brushing

SERVES 4

37

1 Trim any skin from the tuna. Place the steaks in a single layer in a shallow dish. Sprinkle over the lime rind and juice, olive oil, salt and pepper. Cover and chill until required.

2 Make the pepper purée. Brush the peppers with oil and grill, skin-side down, on a hot barbecue until the skin blisters and blackens. Cook the unpeeled onion on the barbecue until the skin starts to blacken and the flesh softens, turning occasionally.

3 Put the peppers and onion in a bowl, cover with kitchen paper and cool for 10 minutes, then remove the skins. Process the onion and pepper flesh with the garlic, chillies, bread and oil until smooth. Remove the seeds from the chillies if you prefer a milder flavour. Scrape into a bowl and add salt to taste.

4 Lift the tuna steaks from the marinade and grill them on a hot barbecue for 8–10 minutes. Serve with the pepper purée and lime wedges.

Mexican Barbecued Salmon

INGREDIENTS

1 small red onion
1 garlic clove
6 plum tomatoes
25g / 1oz / 2 tbsp butter
45ml / 3 tbsp tomato ketchup
30ml / 2 tbsp Dijon mustard
30ml / 2 tbsp soft dark brown sugar
15ml / 1 tbsp clear honey
5ml / 1 tsp cayenne pepper
15ml / 1 tbsp ancho chilli powder
15ml / 1 tbsp paprika
15ml / 1 tbsp Worcestershire sauce
4 salmon fillets, about 175g / 6oz each
fresh coriander sprigs, to garnish

SERVES 4

1 Finely chop the red onion and garlic and mix them in a bowl. Dice the tomatoes and keep them separate from the onion mixture.

2 Melt the butter in a large, heavy-based saucepan. Add the onion and garlic and cook for 8–10 minutes. Add the tomatoes and simmer for 15 minutes.

3 Stir in the tomato ketchup, mustard, brown sugar, honey, spices and Worcestershire sauce. Mix well. Bring to the boil, lower the heat and simmer for 20 minutes. Purée the mixture in a food processor, then scrape into a bowl and leave to cool.

4 Spread the salmon fillets on a plate and brush them with the sauce. Cover and chill for at least 2 hours. Grill over a moderately hot barbecue for 2–3 minutes on each side. Garnish with fresh coriander sprigs and serve with any remaining sauce.

COOK'S TIP

Try the sauce with barbecued sausages or as a hamburger relish. It would also make a good alternative marinade for the tiger prawn skewers in this book.

Tiger Prawns with Walnut Pesto

INGREDIENTS

12–16 large tiger prawns, in the shell
WALNUT PESTO
50g/2oz/½ cup walnut pieces
60ml/4 tbsp chopped fresh flat leaf parsley
60ml/4 tbsp shredded fresh basil
2 garlic cloves, chopped
45ml/3 tbsp grated Parmesan cheese
30ml/2 tbsp extra virgin olive oil
30ml/2 tbsp walnut oil
salt and ground black pepper

SERVES 4

40

2 Combine the walnuts, parsley, basil, garlic and Parmesan in a food processor. Add both types of oil and grind to a paste. Scrape the paste into a bowl and season with salt and pepper.

3 Add half the pesto to the prawns. Toss to coat, then replace the cover. Marinate for about an hour at room temperature, or overnight in the fridge.

4 Soak 8 short bamboo skewers in cold water for 30 minutes. Drain and thread with the prawns. Cook on a moderately hot barbecue for 4–6 minutes. Serve with the remaining pesto.

1 Peel the prawns. Remove the heads, but leave the tails intact. Remove the veins. Put the prawns into a large bowl, cover and set aside while you make the pesto.

Barbecued Stuffed Calamari

INGREDIENTS

500g / 1¼lb baby squid
1 garlic clove, crushed
3 plum tomatoes, peeled and chopped
8 drained sun-dried tomatoes in oil, chopped
60ml / 4 tbsp shredded fresh basil,
plus extra to serve
60ml / 4 tbsp fresh white breadcrumbs
15ml / 1 tbsp red wine vinegar
45ml / 3 tbsp olive oil
salt and ground black pepper
lemon juice, to serve

SERVES 4

1 Prepare each squid by holding the body in one hand and gently pulling away the head and tentacles. Discard the head; chop the tentacles roughly. Keeping the body sac whole, remove the transparent "quill" from inside, then peel off the brown skin on the outside. Rub a little salt into each squid and wash well under cold water.

2 Mix the chopped squid, garlic, plum tomatoes, sun-dried tomatoes, basil and breadcrumbs in a bowl. Stir in the vinegar, with 30ml/2 tbsp of the oil. Add plenty of salt and pepper and mix well. Soak cocktail sticks (as many as there are squid) in water for 10 minutes.

3 Fill the squid with the stuffing, closing the ends with the drained cocktail sticks. Brush with the remaining oil and grill over a moderately hot barbecue

for 4–5 minutes, turning frequently. Sprinkle with lemon juice and extra basil to serve.

41

Grilled Sardines with Herb Salsa

INGREDIENTS

12–16 fresh sardines, cleaned
oil, for brushing
juice of 1 lemon
HERB SALSA
15g/½oz/1 tbsp butter
4 spring onions, chopped
1 garlic clove, crushed
30ml/2 tbsp finely chopped fresh parsley
30ml/2 tbsp finely snipped fresh chives
30ml/2 tbsp finely shredded fresh basil
30ml/2 tbsp green olive paste
10ml/2 tsp balsamic vinegar
grated rind of 1 lemon
salt and ground black pepper

42

SERVES 4

1 Rinse the sardines and dry them thoroughly with kitchen paper. Arrange the fish on a grill rack or on one half of a hinged grill.

2 Make the herb salsa. Melt the butter in a saucepan. Add the spring onions and garlic and cook over a low heat for 2 minutes, shaking the pan occasionally, until softened but not browned.

3 Stir in the herbs, olive paste, vinegar and lemon rind. Season to taste. Mix well. Cover the pan and keep it warm on the edge of the barbecue.

4 Brush the sardines lightly with oil. Sprinkle with lemon juice, salt and pepper. Grill over a moderately hot barbecue for 2 minutes on each side. Serve with the warm salsa and offer chunks of crusty bread, for mopping up the tasty juices.

Thai Spiced Fish

INGREDIENTS

*4 red snapper or mullet, about 350g/12oz
each, cleaned and scaled
banana leaves or heavy-duty foil, for wrapping
1 lime, halved
1 garlic clove, thinly sliced
2 spring onions, thinly sliced
30ml/2 tbsp Thai red curry paste
60ml/4 tbsp coconut milk*

SERVES 4

43

I Cut several deep slashes in the side of each fish. Place each fish on a layer of banana leaves or a piece of foil large enough to enclose it. Slice one lime half and tuck the slices into the slashes in the fish, with slivers of garlic. Scatter the spring onions over the fish.

2 Grate the rind and squeeze the juice from the remaining half-lime. Combine both in a bowl and stir in the curry paste and coconut milk. Mix well, then spoon evenly over the fish.

3 Wrap the leaves over the fish to enclose each one completely. Tie firmly with string. Grill on a moderately hot barbecue for 15–20 minutes, turning occasionally. Check one portion to make sure the fish is thoroughly cooked through, then serve all the fish in their wrappings, inviting guests to open them at the table.

Barbecued Scallops with Fennel & Lime

INGREDIENTS

1 fennel bulb
2 limes
12 large scallops, shelled
1 egg yolk
75g / 3oz / 6 tbsp butter, melted
oil, for brushing
salt and ground black pepper

SERVES 4

44

1 Trim any feathery leaves from the fennel and set them aside. Slice the fennel bulb lengthways into thick wedges. Cut one lime into wedges. Grate the rind of the remaining lime, then squeeze the juice.

2 Put the scallops in a bowl and pour over half the lime juice and half the grated rind. Toss to coat. Put the remaining lime rind and juice in a separate bowl.

Add the egg yolk and whisk until pale and smooth.

3 Gradually whisk in the melted butter and continue whisking until the sauce is thick and smooth. Finely chop the reserved fennel leaves and stir them in, with salt and pepper to taste.

4 Brush the fennel wedges with oil. Cook them on a hot barbecue for 3–4 minutes, turning once. Add the scallops (placing them on a cooler area of the grill) and cook for 3–4 minutes more, turning once. Garnish with the lime wedges and serve with the lime and fennel sauce.

COOK'S TIP
If you can only obtain small scallops, use 16–20 and thread them on flat skewers so that they can be turned more easily.

Vegetables &
Vegetarian Dishes

Potato Skewers with Mustard Dip

INGREDIENTS

1kg / 2½lb small new potatoes
200g / 7oz shallots, halved
30ml / 2 tbsp olive oil
15ml / 1 tbsp sea salt
MUSTARD DIP
4 garlic cloves, crushed
2 egg yolks
30ml / 2 tbsp lemon juice
300ml / ½ pint / 1¼ cups extra virgin olive oil
10ml / 2 tsp whole-grain mustard
salt and ground black pepper

SERVES 4

3 Brush the potatoes and shallots with oil and sprinkle with a little sea salt. Cook for 10–12 minutes over a hot barbecue, turning occasionally, until the

potatoes and shallots are tender. Serve at once with the mustard dip.

47

1 Make the dip. Combine the garlic, egg yolks and lemon juice in a blender or food processor. Whizz for a few seconds until smooth. With the motor running, add the oil very gradually, pouring it through the cap or feeder tube in a thin stream, until the mixture forms a thick, glossy cream. Add the mustard and season with salt and pepper.

2 Bring a large saucepan of lightly salted water to the boil. Add the potatoes and par-boil them for 5 minutes. Drain well, then thread with the shallots on to four metal skewers.

Red Bean & Mushroom Burgers

INGREDIENTS

15ml/1 tbsp olive oil
1 small onion, finely chopped
1 garlic clove, crushed
5ml/1 tsp ground cumin
5ml/1 tsp ground coriander
2.5ml/½ tsp ground turmeric
115g/4oz/1 cup mushrooms, finely chopped
400g/14oz can red kidney beans
30ml/2 tbsp chopped fresh coriander
wholemeal flour (optional)
olive oil, for brushing
salt and ground black pepper
warmed pitta breads, lettuce and
cherry tomatoes, to serve

SERVES 4

1 Heat the oil in a wide, shallow pan. Fry the onion and garlic over a moderate heat for about 5 minutes, until softened. Add the spices and cook for 1 minute more, stirring constantly.

2 Add the mushrooms. Raise the heat and cook for about 7 minutes, stirring frequently, until they are tender and dry. Remove the pan from the heat.

3 Drain the beans, tip them into a bowl and mash with a fork. Add to the mushroom mixture, with the fresh coriander, mixing thoroughly. Season with plenty of salt and pepper.

4 With floured hands, form the mixture into four flat burgers. If the mixture is too sticky to handle, mix in a little wholemeal flour. Brush the burgers

lightly with oil and cook on a hot barbecue for 8–10 minutes, turning once, until golden brown. These burgers are not as firm as meat burgers, so handle them gently on the barbecue. Serve with warmed pitta breads, lettuce and cherry tomatoes. A spoonful of Greek-style yogurt makes a welcome addition.

48

Grilled Aubergine & Feta Rolls

INGREDIENTS

2 large aubergines
olive oil
10–12 drained sun-dried tomatoes in oil
handful of large, fresh basil leaves
150g/5oz/scant 1 cup feta cheese
salt and ground black pepper
fresh basil sprigs, to garnish

SERVES 4

50

1 Slice the aubergines lengthways into 5mm/ ¼in slices. Sprinkle with salt and layer in a colander. Leave to drain for about 30 minutes.

2 Rinse the aubergines under cold running water, drain and pat dry with kitchen paper. Brush both sides of each slice with oil. Grill on a hot barbecue for 2–3 minutes, turning once, until tender and golden brown.

3 Arrange the sun-dried toma-toes over one end of each aubergine slice. Add the fresh basil leaves. Cut the feta cheese into short sticks and place on top. Season with salt and ground black pepper.

4 Roll the aubergine slices around to enclose the filling. Cook the rolls on the barbecue for 2–3 minutes, until heated through. Garnish with fresh basil sprigs and serve with slices of ciabatta or chunky wholemeal bread.

VARIATION
Use tofu instead of feta cheese, if you like. For extra flavour, sprinkle the tofu with a little soy sauce before wrapping.

Brie Parcels with Almonds

INGREDIENTS

4 large drained vine leaves in brine
200g/7oz piece of Brie cheese
30ml/2 tbsp snipped fresh chives
25g/1oz/¼ cup ground almonds
5ml/1 tsp crushed black peppercorns
15ml/1 tbsp olive oil, plus extra for brushing
30ml/2 tbsp flaked almonds

SERVES 2–4

3 Bring the stem end of each vine leaf up over the filling, then fold in the sides and top to enclose the filling completely and make a neat parcel. Brush the parcels

with oil and cook on a hot barbecue for 3–4 minutes, until the cheese has begun to melt. Serve at once, with crusty bread.

51

1 Rinse the vine leaves under cold water. Drain and dry on sheets of kitchen paper. Spread the leaves out on a board. Cut the Brie into four chunks and

place each chunk on a vine leaf.

2 Mix the fresh chives, ground almonds, peppercorns and oil in a bowl. Place a spoonful of the mixture over the Brie on each leaf. Sprinkle with the flaked almonds.

Grilled Mediterranean Vegetables

INGREDIENTS

2 aubergines
2 large courgettes
1 red pepper
1 yellow pepper
1 fennel bulb
1 red onion
olive oil, for brushing
salt and ground black pepper
SAUCE
150ml/¼ pint/⅔ cup
Greek-style yogurt
45ml/3 tbsp pesto

SERVES 4

COOK'S TIP

*Baby vegetables are perfect for cooking on
the barbecue. If using baby aubergines,
simply slice them in half lengthways.
They will not need to be salted.*

52

1 Cut the aubergines into 1cm/½in rounds. Sprinkle with salt and layer in a colander. Leave to drain for about 30 minutes, then rinse well under cold water, drain and pat dry with kitchen paper.

2 Cut the courgettes in half lengthways. Cut the peppers in half, leaving the stalks on. Remove the seeds. Slice the fennel and onion into thick wedges.

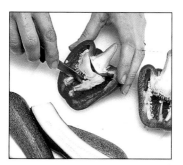

3 Make the sauce by swirling the yogurt and pesto together to create a marbled effect. Spoon the sauce into a serving bowl.

4 Then arrange the vegetables on the hot barbecue. Brush with oil and sprinkle with salt and pepper. Grill them until lightly browned, turning occasionally. The aubergines and peppers will take 6–8 minutes to cook; the onion and fennel 4–5 minutes. Serve with the marbled pesto sauce.

Grilled Herb Polenta with Tomatoes

INGREDIENTS

olive oil, for greasing
750ml / 1¼ pints / 3 cups vegetable stock
or water
5ml / 1 tsp salt (optional)
175g / 6oz / 1 cup polenta
25g / 1oz / 2 tbsp butter
75ml / 5 tbsp mixed chopped fresh herbs (parsley, chives and basil), plus extra to garnish
4 large plum or beefsteak tomatoes, halved
salt and ground black pepper

SERVES 4

54

1 Prepare the polenta several hours before you plan to have the barbecue. Grease a shallow baking dish lightly with oil and set it aside. Pour the stock or water into a large saucepan, add salt if needed, and bring to the boil. Lower the heat and add the polenta, stirring constantly.

2 Continue to stir over a moderate heat for 5 minutes, until the polenta thickens and starts to come away from the sides of the pan. Remove from the heat and stir in the butter and herbs, with black pepper to taste.

3 Tip the mixture into the prepared baking dish and spread it out evenly. Allow to stand until the mixture has cooled and set. Turn out the polenta and stamp out rounds with a biscuit cutter.

4 Brush the tomato halves with olive oil and sprinkle with salt and ground black pepper. Grill the tomatoes and polenta rounds on a moderately hot barbecue for 5 minutes, turning once. Garnish with the chopped fresh herbs and serve at once.

Baked Squash with Parmesan

INGREDIENTS

2 acorn or butternut squash,
about 450g/1lb each
15ml/1 tbsp olive oil
50g/2oz/¼ cup butter, softened
75g/3oz/1 cup grated Parmesan cheese, plus
extra to serve
60ml/4 tbsp pine nuts, toasted
2.5ml/½ tsp grated nutmeg
salt and ground black pepper

SERVES 4

1 Cut the squash in half. Scoop out the seeds and rinse the flesh with cold water. Brush the cut surfaces with oil and sprinkle the flesh with salt and pepper.

2 Wrap each squash in a double layer of heavy-duty foil and place in the embers of the barbecue fire. Cook for 25–30 minutes or until tender, turning occasionally to ensure that the squash cook evenly.

3 Carefully lift the squash out of the embers and unwrap them from the foil. Scoop out the flesh into a bowl, keeping the shells intact. Dice the flesh, then stir in the softened butter, Parmesan and pine nuts, with salt and pepper to taste.

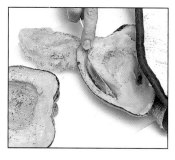

4 Spoon the mixture back into the squash shells, sprinkle with any remaining Parmesan and the grated nutmeg and serve at once.

55

Desserts

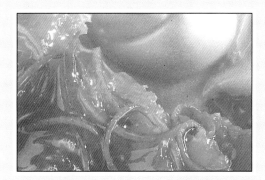

Pineapple Wedges with Rum Butter Glaze

INGREDIENTS

1 pineapple
30ml/2 tbsp dark muscovado sugar
5ml/1 tsp ground ginger
50g/2oz/¼ cup butter, melted
30ml/2 tbsp dark rum

SERVES 4

1 Soak 4 bamboo skewers in cold water for 30 minutes. Using a large, sharp knife, cut the pineapple in half, and then in half again, to give four wedges, each with a section of stalk and leaves. Cut out and discard the core from each wedge.

2 Cut between the flesh and skin, to release the flesh without actually lifting it away. Leaving the flesh on the skin, slice it across into chunks. Drain the skewers, 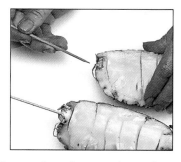 then push each skewer lengthways through a pineapple wedge and into the stalk, to hold the chunks in place.

3 Mix the sugar, ginger, melted butter and rum in a cup or bowl. Brush some of the the mixture over the pineapple. Grill on a hot barbecue for 3–4 minutes. Serve on individual plates, with the remaining rum mixture poured over.

COOK'S TIP
For an easier version, remove the skin and cut the pineapple into thick rounds. Remove the cores with an apple corer.

Char-grilled Apples on Cinnamon Toasts

INGREDIENTS

4 sweet eating apples
juice of ½ lemon
30ml/2 tbsp golden caster sugar
5ml/1 tsp ground cinnamon
4 individual brioches or muffins
50g/2oz/¼ cup butter, melted
clotted cream or Greek-style yogurt, to serve

SERVES 4

1 Core the apples, but do not peel them. Cut each apple horizontally into three or four rings and place in a shallow dish. Sprinkle lemon juice over the top

of the rings. Mix the sugar and cinnamon in a small bowl and set aside.

2 Cut the brioches or muffins into thick slices. Brush them with melted butter on both sides, then place them on a hot barbecue, with the apple rings. Cook for 3–4 minutes, until the apples are cooked through and the brioches or muffins are toasted.

3 Sprinkle half of the cinnamon sugar evenly over the cooked apple rings and toasted brioche or muffin slices, and cook for 1 minute more, until the topping turns a rich golden brown.

4 Arrange the apple rings on top of the toasted brioche or muffin slices to serve. Sprinkle the rest of the cinnamon sugar over and add a generous spoonful of clotted cream or Greek-style yogurt. Serve at once.

Baked Bananas with Vanilla Butter

INGREDIENTS

4 bananas
seeds from 6 green cardamom pods
1 vanilla pod
finely grated rind of 1 small orange
30ml / 2 tbsp brandy or orange juice
60ml / 4 tbsp light muscovado sugar
40g / 1½oz / 3 tbsp butter, melted
crème fraîche or Greek-style yogurt, to serve

SERVES 4

60

1 Place the bananas, in their skins, on the hot barbecue. Leave for 6–8 minutes, turning occasionally, until the skins are blackened all over.

2 Meanwhile, tip the cardamom seeds into a mortar and crush lightly with a pestle. Split the vanilla pod lengthways and scrape the tiny seeds into the mortar. Grind lightly, then mix in the orange rind, brandy or orange juice, sugar and butter, to make a thick paste.

3 Slit the skin of each banana, open out slightly, and spoon in a little of the spiced vanilla butter. Serve at once, with a generous spoonful of crème fraîche or Greek-style yogurt.

VARIATIONS

Children love these with maple syrup or melted chocolate instead of vanilla butter. For their parents, try drizzling liqueur over the bananas.

Nectarines with Marzipan & Mascarpone

INGREDIENTS

4 firm, ripe nectarines or peaches
75g/3oz marzipan
75g/3oz/5 tbsp mascarpone cheese
3 macaroon biscuits, crushed

SERVES 4

3 Place the filled nectarine or peach halves on a hot barbecue. Cook for 3–5 minutes, until they are hot and the mascarpone has begun to melt. Serve at once.

VARIATIONS

Marzipan makes the perfect filling for barbecued fruits. It softens as it cooks, and flavours the fruit beautifully. Try it as a filling for baked apples: mix in a little icing sugar and some sultanas, fill the apples and top each one with a few flakes of butter. Wrap in heavy-duty foil and bake for about 20 minutes on a moderately hot barbecue.

61

I Cut the nectarines or peaches in half and remove the stones. Cut the marzipan into eight pieces. Use your hands to press one piece into the stone cavity of each nectarine or peach half.

2 Spoon the mascarpone cheese on top of the marzipan pieces. Then sprinkle the crushed macaroons over the mascarpone.

Oranges in Cointreau & Maple Syrup

INGREDIENTS

25g/1oz/2 tbsp butter, melted
4 oranges
30ml/2 tbsp maple syrup
30ml/2 tbsp Cointreau or Grand Marnier
liqueur
crème fraîche or fromage frais, to serve

SERVES 4

62

1 Cut eight identical squares of foil, each large enough to wrap an orange. Double up the squares for extra strength, then brush the centre of each with

a little of the melted butter.

2 Carefully pare the rind from one orange. Using a sharp knife, scrape off any pith, then cut the rind into matchstick strips. Place the rind in a small saucepan, add water to cover and bring to the boil. Cook for 5 minutes, then drain the strips and set them aside.

3 Peel all the oranges, keeping them whole and taking care to remove all the pith. Working over a bowl to catch the juice, slice them crossways into several thick slices. Reassemble each orange and place it on a square of doubled foil.

4 Then tuck the foil around each orange, leaving the foil open at the top. Stir the maple syrup and liqueur into the orange juice, then spoon the mixture over

the oranges. Add a dab of butter and close the foil to seal in the juices.

5 Place the parcels on a hot barbecue and cook for 10–12 minutes until hot. Serve with crème fraîche or fromage frais, topped with shreds of blanched orange rind.

COOK'S TIP

For an alcohol-free version of this delicious dessert, substitute a golden shred marmalade for the Cointreau liqueur.

Barbecued Strawberry Croissants

INGREDIENTS

4 croissants
115g/4oz/½ cup ricotta cheese
115g/4oz/8 tbsp strawberry conserve or jam

SERVES 4

I Split the croissants in half and open them out on a board. Spread the bottom half of each croissant with ricotta cheese.

2 Top the bottom half of each croissant with a generous spoonful of strawberry conserve, spreading it evenly. Replace the top half of each croissant.

3 Place the filled croissants on a hot barbecue and cook for 2–3 minutes, turning once. Serve the croissants at once, on their own or with ice-cream.

VARIATIONS

• Fresh scones, muffins or teacakes can be toasted on the barbecue as an alternative to croissants.
• Vary the filling. Cream cheese or mascarpone can be used instead of ricotta and apricot or black cherry jam used instead of strawberry.
• Sprinkle chocolate chips inside the croissants for a barbecued version of pain au chocolat.

Fruit Kebabs with Chocolate & Marshmallow Fondue

INGREDIENTS

2 bananas
2 kiwi fruit
12 strawberries
15g / ½oz / 1 tbsp butter, melted
15ml / 1 tbsp lemon juice
5ml / 1 tsp ground cinnamon
FONDUE
225g / 8oz plain chocolate, broken into squares
120ml / 4fl oz / ½ cup single cream
8 marshmallows
2.5ml / ½ tsp vanilla essence

SERVES 4

1 Soak four bamboo skewers in cold water for 30 minutes. Peel the bananas and cut each one into four thick chunks. Peel and quarter the kiwi fruit.

2 Drain the skewers and thread them with the bananas, kiwi fruit and strawberries. Mix the butter, lemon juice and cinnamon in a small bowl and brush the mixture over the fruit on the skewers.

3 Make the fondue. Combine the chocolate, cream and marshmallows in a small pan. Heat gently on the barbecue, stirring until the mixture has melted and is smooth. Do not allow the mixture to approach boiling point.

4 Move the fondue to the edge of the barbecue to keep warm. Meanwhile, cook the fruit kebabs for 2–3 minutes, turning once. Stir the vanilla essence into the fondue and serve it with the kebabs.

65

Part Two
Perfect Picnics

Fresh air sharpens the appetite and a picnic basket
filled with tempting fare will be doubly rewarding after
a hard day's exploring. Here are recipes for fabulous
feasts that will transform any outing into a truly
memorable event.

Introduction

Pack up a picnic and pursue one of life's most delightful pleasures. Despite – or because of – the vagaries of the weather and the other uncertainties associated with eating out, such as whether the midges will be massing or the ants preparing for an all-out assault, eating out of doors never fails to be an adventure. Whether you stick a few sandwiches and a couple of apples in a backpack, or spread out a banquet by a babbling brook, there's always something special about eating in the open air.

The Victorians loved a lavish picnic and thought nothing of toting to the site huge, groaning hampers containing everything from whole joints of roast meat, dressed crab and lobster, salads and savouries to elaborate puddings and cakes.

The traditional Victorian picnic feast would include the obligatory cucumber sandwiches followed by cricket and croquet, with games for the children and adults dozing in the warm afternoon sunshine.

The advent of the barbecue pushed picnics into second place for a while, but in recent years there has been a revival and today picnics are being appreciated more and more as a wonderful way of combining social entertaining with enjoyment of the countryside. Kitchenware companies have been quick to appreciate this, and there is now a vast range of equipment available to the dedicated picnicker. There seems to be a suitable container for every type and shape of food, some with separate compartments for sauces and dressings, and chiller boxes and bags to carry them in. Unbreakable steel flasks are invaluable for hot and cold drinks; choose a wide-mouthed flask for soups to make pouring that much easier.

While such equipment is by no means essential, it can make a huge difference to the success of your picnic. If you foresee no handy stream to cool your champagne in, pack it in a special insulated bag, and when pouring the champagne, avoid spills by using spiked wine glasses that stick firmly in the ground. Picnic tableware should be bright and colourful to compete with the glories of nature. Have place settings in individual colours for each guest, to make plates and knives more easily identifiable.

A good idea is to pack plenty of cushions and back-rests – there's nothing worse than trying to eat a meal when you are horribly uncomfortable – and pack a couple of garden chairs for older guests. Picnic rugs are pretty, but often too small for a large crowd. An old bedsheet may be more practical, and will certainly be easier to wash. Spread a few bin bags underneath it to keep the worst of the damp and dirt at bay, then use the bags for taking away your rubbish when the picnic is over.

Better insulated containers may have improved food safety, but there's no room for complacency. There's little point in carefully keeping food chilled if you later leave it standing in the sunshine for several hours. Pack any uneaten food away quickly: you can always get it out again.

Always take care to leave the picnic site as pristine as possible. Make fires only in designated areas, and if you light candles for illumination or to keep insects away, make sure they can't be knocked over.

Most of all, you should sit back, relax and enjoy the delicious food and the company. That's the real enjoyment of eating out!

Perfect Picnic Fare

BREADS

The original convenience food. Bake your own – it's so simple with easy-blend dried yeast – or raid the bakery. Baps and bagels become sophisticated snacks with interesting fillings, and pitta pockets are perfect for holding falafel or salads.

CAKES AND BAKES

It is best to avoid gooey icings but fruit cakes and loaves are ideal. Pack them in the tin in which they were baked.

CRUDITÉS

Pack a selection of crisp raw vegetables, cut into slim sticks or strips or broken into florets. Include carrots, radishes, cauliflower, peppers of every colour, spring onions, firm baby button mushrooms and cucumber. Serve with hummus, taramasalata or tzatziki.

DESSERTS

Light, fresh and pretty – that's the only recipe for the perfect picnic dessert. Avoid anything too fragile, and keep cream-based puddings well chilled.

DRESSINGS

Pack oil-based dressings in leakproof beakers and shake just before adding to salads. Use bought mayonnaise for picnics, rather than making your own.

DRINKS

It is easy to underestimate how much people drink in the open air. Take plenty of fruit juices and bottled water as well as wine and beer for non-drivers, if wanted. Use unbreakable flasks for hot drinks like coffee, tea or hot chocolate.

FRUIT

Fresh berry fruits, packed in baskets (with leaves), look lovely for a summer picnic.

PASTRIES

Individual pastries, like tartlets, pasties and filo kerchiefs, are easy to eat, and you can include several different fillings. A large pie makes an impressive centrepiece.

PÂTÉS

A rough country pâté is a good addition to the feast, but must be kept chilled. Avoid chicken liver pâté, which is too perishable.

PIZZAS

For a quick and easy treat, make up a batch of pizza dough and cut out small rounds with biscuit cutters. Spread with home-made tomato sauce, add the topping of your choice, then sprinkle with a mixture of grated Cheddar and mozzarella. Bake at 220°C/425°F/Gas 7 for 15 minutes.

SALADS

Made for outdoor eating, salads can be simple or elaborate. Garnishes, croûtons and sprinkles (like toasted nuts or seeds) are easy to pack and turn a simple salad into something special.

SOUPS

Cold soups, such as gazpacho or vichyssoise, are ideal for a hot day, whereas winter looks a shade warmer when viewed over a steaming cup of minestrone. Transport soups in wide-mouthed flasks and include bowls and spoons.

71

CHECKLIST

- Corkscrew
- Napkins
- Salt and pepper
- Kitchen paper
- Damp flannels or wipes
- Chopping board
- Serving spoons and lifters
- Knives for food preparation
- Sunscreen
- Insect repellent
- Bin bags

Techniques

PREPARING SALAD LEAVES

Wash and drain the leaves. Break off any tough ribs. Dry robust leaves in a salad spinner; blot delicate leaves with kitchen paper. Pack the leaves into polythene bags, close tightly and store in the fridge before packing in a chiller bag.

MIXING BLUE CHEESE DRESSING

Remove the rind from 75g/3oz Stilton and crumble the cheese into a bowl. Beat in 150ml/¼ pint/⅔ cup natural yogurt, with 45ml/3 tbsp olive oil and 30ml/2 tbsp lemon juice. Sprinkle with fresh chives. Season well.

MAKING FRENCH DRESSING

Mix 90ml/6 tbsp extra-virgin olive oil and 15ml/1 tbsp white wine vinegar in a screw-top jar. Add 5ml/1 tsp French mustard and a pinch of caster sugar. Close the jar tightly and shake well. Shake again before dressing the salad.

MAKING GARLIC CROÛTONS

Cut the crusts off 3 slices of day-old bread; slice the bread into small cubes. Heat 60ml/4 tbsp olive oil in a frying pan and fry the shapes until crisp and golden. Sprinkle with salt and drain on kitchen paper. Pack in an airtight tub.

Simple Sandwich Fillings

AVOCADO & SPRING ONION
Cut an avocado in half and remove the stone and peel. Mash the flesh until smooth, then beat in 1 chopped spring onion and 10ml/ 2 tsp lemon juice. Season with a dash of Worcestershire sauce and then add plenty of salt and pepper.

TUNA & TOMATO
Drain a 75g/3oz can of tuna. Flake the fish with a fork. Add 25g/1oz/2 tbsp softened butter, 15ml/1 tbsp tomato ketchup and 15ml/1 tbsp mayonnaise. Mix well, then add salt and pepper to taste.

EGG & CRESS
Shell 2 hard-boiled eggs and chop them finely. Add 50g/2oz/¼ cup full-fat soft cheese and 30ml/2 tbsp mayonnaise. Mix well, then snip in the tops from a carton of mustard and cress. Season well with salt and pepper.

ONION WITH SPINACH & CHEESE
Chop an onion and fry in olive oil until golden. Allow to cool. Layer the onion on granary baps with raw spinach leaves and grated Cheddar cheese mixed with a little mayonnaise.

SMOKED SALMON & GRAVLAX SAUCE
Mix 25g/1oz/2 tbsp butter with 5ml/1 tsp grated lemon zest and spread over 4 slices of rye bread. Cover with 100g/4oz smoked salmon and add a curly endive leaf and a lemon slice. Spoon over 60ml/4 tbsp Gravlax Sauce. Garnish each portion with a sprig of fresh dill.

FRANKFURTER & POTATO SALAD
Mix 115g/4oz/⅔ cup potato salad with 2 finely chopped spring onions. Use as a sandwich filling with 2 sliced frankfurters and 2 sliced tomatoes.

PARMA HAM, PESTO & MOZZARELLA
Stir 30ml/2 tbsp pesto into 60ml/4 tbsp mayonnaise. Use as a filling for bridge rolls, adding sliced Parma ham, mozzarella and vine tomatoes. Add some shredded fresh basil, if you like.

Finger Food

Falafel

INGREDIENTS

150g/5oz/¾ cup dried chick-peas
1 large onion, roughly chopped
2 garlic cloves, roughly chopped
60ml/4 tbsp roughly chopped fresh parsley
5ml/1 tsp ground cumin
5ml/1 tsp ground coriander
2.5ml/½ tsp baking powder
oil for deep-frying
salt and ground black pepper
pitta bread, salad and yogurt, to serve

SERVES 4

1 Put the chick-peas in a large bowl with enough cold water to cover. Leave to soak overnight.

2 Drain the chick-peas and put them in a saucepan. Add fresh water to cover, bring to the boil and boil rapidly for 10 minutes. Lower the heat and simmer for 1–1½ hours until the chick-peas are tender. Drain well.

3 Tip the chick-peas into a food processor. Add the chopped onion, garlic, fresh parsley, spices and baking powder, with salt and pepper to taste. Process to a firm paste.

4 Shape the mixture into walnut-size balls using your hands, and then flatten them slightly. Heat the oil for deep-frying in a large saucepan and fry the falafel

in batches until golden. Drain on kitchen paper and allow to cool completely. Wrap in several layers of foil for transporting to the picnic, and serve with pitta bread, salad and yogurt.

Pan Bagna

INGREDIENTS

1 extra-long French stick
150ml / ¼ pint / ⅔ cup French Dressing
1 small onion, thinly sliced
3 tomatoes, sliced
1 small green or red pepper, seeded and sliced
50g / 2oz can anchovy fillets, drained
and halved
90g / 3½oz can tuna in oil, drained
and flaked
50g / 2oz / ⅓ cup stoned black olives, halved

SERVES 4–6

1 Split the French stick horizontally along one side, without cutting all the way through the crust. Open the bread out and sprinkle the French dressing evenly over both cut surfaces.

2 Then arrange the onion, tomatoes, pepper, anchovies, tuna and olives on the bottom half of the stick. Re-form by pressing the halves firmly together.

3 Wrap the filled stick in clear film, lay a board on top and add several weights along the length of the sandwich (cans of fruit or vegetables work well). Leave for 1 hour so that the dressing soaks into the bread.

4 Remove the weights and board, then wrap the pan bagna in double foil for taking to the picnic. Cut into sections to serve.

76

Fennel & Lavender Tarts

INGREDIENTS

175g/6oz shortcrust pastry, thawed if frozen
FILLING
75g/3oz/6 tbsp butter
1 large Spanish onion, finely sliced
1 fennel bulb, trimmed and sliced
30ml/2 tbsp fresh lavender florets or 15ml/
1 tbsp dried culinary lavender, finely chopped
150ml/¼ pint/⅔ cup crème fraîche
2 egg yolks
salt and ground black pepper

SERVES 4

1 Roll out the pastry on a lightly floured surface and line four 7.5cm/3in loose-based individual flan tins. Prick the bottom of each pastry case with a fork and chill.

2 Preheat the oven to 200°C/400°F/ Gas 6. Make the filling. Melt the butter in a sauce-pan and soften the onion and fennel with the lavender over a low heat.

3 Line the pastry cases with greaseproof paper and bake blind for 5 minutes, then remove the paper and bake for 4 minutes more. Lower the oven temperature to 180°C/350°F/Gas 4.

4 Mix the crème fraîche and egg yolks in a jug and add salt and pepper to taste. Divide the onion mixture among the pastry cases, pour the crème fraîche mixture on top and bake for 10–15 minutes, until the filling has set. When cold, pack carefully in a rigid tub, adding a few extra lavender flowers, for garnishing.

Country-style Pork & Leek Pâté

INGREDIENTS

15g / ½oz / 1 tbsp butter
450g / 1lb leeks, trimmed and sliced
2–3 large garlic cloves, crushed
*150g / 5oz rindless smoked streaky
bacon rashers*
1kg / 2¼lb lean pork leg or shoulder, cubed
7.5ml / 1½ tsp chopped fresh thyme
3 fresh sage leaves, finely chopped
1.5ml / ¼ tsp ground cumin
1.5ml / ¼ tsp grated nutmeg
salt and ground black pepper
1 bay leaf, to garnish

SERVES 8–10

1 Preheat the oven to 180°C/350°F/ Gas 4. Melt the butter in a large frying pan. Add the leeks, cover and cook gently for 10 minutes. Stir in the garlic

and cook for 10 minutes more until the leeks are very soft. Set aside.

2 Reserve 2 bacon rashers. Grind the rest with the pork to a coarse purée by pulsing the mixture in small batches in a food processor. Scrape into a bowl and remove any white stringy bits. Add the leeks, herbs and spices to the bowl, with plenty of salt and pepper. Mix well.

3 Line a 1.5 litre/2½ pint/6¼ cup terrine with non-stick baking paper. Spoon in the pork mixture, pressing it down firmly into the corners. Tap the tin to settle the mixture, smooth the surface and arrange the reserved bacon and bay leaf on top. Cover tightly with foil.

4 Place the terrine in a roasting pan and pour in boiling water to come halfway up the sides. Bake in the oven for 1¼ hours, then carefully pour away the water. Leaving the terrine in the pan, place a board and weights (cans of fruit or vegetables work well) on top to compress the pâté as it cools. Chill in the fridge overnight, then remove the board and weights. Wrap the pâté carefully and transport to the picnic site in a chiller bag. Serve with large chunks of wholemeal bread.

Hummus with Tahini

INGREDIENTS

150g / 5oz / ¾ cup chick-peas
juice of 2 lemons
2 garlic cloves, sliced
30ml / 2 tbsp olive oil
pinch of cayenne pepper
150ml / ¼ pint / ⅔ cup tahini paste
extra olive oil and cayenne pepper, for sprinkling
salt and ground black pepper

SERVES 4–6

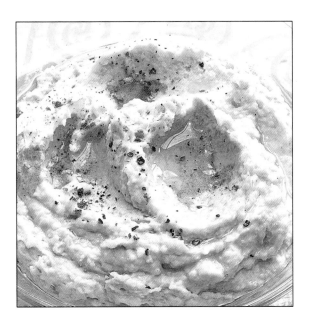

I Put the chick-peas in a large bowl with enough cold water to cover. Leave them to soak overnight.

2 Drain the chick-peas and put them in a saucepan. Add fresh water to cover, bring to the boil and boil rapidly for 10 minutes. Lower the heat and simmer for I–I½ hours until the chick-peas are tender. Drain well.

3 Tip the chick-peas into a food processor. Process to a smooth purée. Add the lemon juice, sliced garlic, olive oil, cayenne pepper and tahini paste. Process the  mixture again until creamy, scraping down the sides of the bowl from time to time, as necessary.

4 Scrape the hummus into a plastic tub and add salt and pepper to taste. Seal the tub tightly and chill until ready to pack for the picnic. If possible, take along a little extra olive oil and cayenne pepper to sprinkle over the surface as a garnish. Hummus makes a delicious snack served with chilled crudités and pitta bread, or simply a couple of bright red radishes.

Potato & Onion Tortilla

INGREDIENTS

300ml / ½ pint / 1¼ cups olive oil
6 large potatoes, sliced
2 Spanish onions, sliced
6 size 2 eggs
salt and ground black pepper
cherry tomatoes, to serve

SERVES 4

1 Heat the oil in a large frying pan. Stir in the potatoes and onions. Sprinkle with a little salt, cover and cook over a gentle heat for 20 minutes until soft.

2 Beat the eggs in a large bowl. Using a slotted spoon, lift the potato and onion slices out of the pan and add to the eggs. Season to taste, then carefully pour off all but 60ml/4 tbsp of the oil remaining in the pan.

3 Then heat the oil again. Add the egg mixture and cook for 2–3 minutes until the base is set. Cover the pan with a plate and carefully invert the tortilla on to it.

Slide it back into the pan and cook for 5 minutes more, until it is golden brown on the outside and moist in the middle.

4 Cool, then wrap in foil and support in a box. Cut into wedges and serve with the cherry tomatoes.

Sun-dried Tomato Bread

INGREDIENTS

45ml/3 tbsp olive oil
1 large onion, finely chopped
400ml/14fl oz/1⅔ cups milk
15ml/1 tbsp tomato purée
675g/1½lb/6 cups strong plain flour
10ml/2 tsp salt
60ml/4 tbsp caster sugar
10g/¼oz sachet easy-blend dried yeast
*75g/3oz/½ cup drained sun-dried tomatoes
in oil, chopped, plus 45ml/3 tbsp oil
from the jar*

MAKES 4 SMALL LOAVES

2 Sift the flour and salt into a mixing bowl. Stir in the sugar and yeast. Make a well in the centre and add the milk mixture, with the contents of the frying pan, the sun-dried tomatoes and their oil. Mix to a soft dough. Knead on a lightly floured surface for 10 minutes until smooth and elastic.

3 Lightly grease a baking sheet. Shape the dough into four rounds and place on the sheet, leaving plenty of room for rising. Cover with a dish towel and leave until the dough has doubled in bulk.

4 Preheat the oven to 220°C/425°F/Gas 7. Bake the loaves for 30 minutes, until they sound hollow when rapped on the bottom. Cool on a wire rack.

1 Heat the olive oil in a small frying pan and fry the onion for 5 minutes over a gentle heat until softened. Set the pan aside. In a saucepan, heat the milk to hand-hot. Pour into a jug and stir in the tomato purée.

COOK'S TIP
The amount of liquid required to make the dough will depend on the absorbency of the flour. Add half the milk mixture at first, then add more as required.

82

Cheese & Chive Scones

INGREDIENTS

115g/4oz/1 cup self-raising white flour
115g/4oz/1 cup self-raising wholemeal flour
2.5ml/½ tsp salt
75g/3oz/½ cup feta cheese
15ml/1 tbsp finely snipped fresh chives
150ml/¼ pint/⅔ cup milk, plus extra for glazing
1.5ml/¼ tsp cayenne pepper

MAKES 9

84

1 Preheat the oven to 200°C/400°F/Gas 6. Sift the flours and salt into a mixing bowl. Tip in any bran remaining in the sieve. Crumble in the feta cheese and rub it into the dry ingredients. Stir in the chives. Working quickly, mix in enough milk to make a soft dough. Knead the dough lightly.

2 Roll or pat out the dough on a floured surface to a thickness of about 2cm/¾in. Using a 6cm/2½in round cutter, cut out about 9 scones.

3 Transfer the scones to a non-stick baking sheet. Brush with milk, then sprinkle with cayenne pepper. Bake for 15 minutes, until golden brown. Allow the

scones to cool on a wire rack, then pack in a tin. Serve with butter, or with a spread made by mixing cream cheese and finely snipped fresh chives.

Dill & Potato Cakes

INGREDIENTS

225g/8oz/2 cups self-raising flour
pinch of salt
40g/1½oz/3 tbsp butter, softened
15ml/1 tbsp finely chopped fresh dill
175g/6oz/1 cup mashed potato, freshly made
30–45ml/2–3 tbsp milk

MAKES 10

1 Preheat the oven to 230°C/450°F/ Gas 8. Grease a large baking sheet. Sift the flour and salt into a mixing bowl. Add the butter and dill. Mix in the mashed potato, with enough milk to make a soft, pliable dough.

2 Roll out the dough on a lightly floured surface. Cut into 10 neat rounds, using a 7.5cm/3in cutter. Place the rounds on the prepared baking sheet and bake for 25 minutes until risen and golden.

3 Allow the cakes to cool on a wire rack, then pack them in a tin. For a special picnic treat, serve with crème fraîche and smoked salmon.

VARIATION

Cheese & Herb Potato Cakes: Stir about 50g/2oz/½ cup crumbled blue cheese into the mashed potato mixture, and substitute fresh chives for the dill. Use 45ml/3 tbsp soured cream instead of the butter.

Salad Days

Tabbouleh with Fennel & Pomegranate

INGREDIENTS

225g / 8oz / 1⅓ cups bulgur wheat
2 fennel bulbs
*1 small fresh red chilli, seeded and
finely chopped*
1 celery stick, finely sliced
6–8 spring onions, chopped
90ml / 6 tbsp chopped fresh mint
90ml / 6 tbsp chopped fresh parsley
seeds from 1 pomegranate
30ml / 2 tbsp olive oil
finely grated rind and juice of 2 lemons
salt and ground black pepper

SERVES 6

2 Cut the fennel bulbs in half and slice them both very thinly. Add to the bulgur, with the chilli, celery, spring onions, fresh herbs and pomegranate seeds. Pour over the olive oil, lemon rind and juice, add salt and pepper to taste and mix well.

3 Pack into a rigid tub for taking to the picnic. Serve with pitta bread and baby cos lettuce leaves. The salad needs to stand for at least 30 minutes before serving.

1 Place the bulgur wheat in a large bowl. Pour over cold water to cover. Leave to stand for 30 minutes, then tip into a sieve lined with muslin or a clean dish  towel. Drain well, then gather up the sides of the cloth and squeeze out as much liquid as possible from the bulgur. Tip it into a bowl.

Ratatouille

INGREDIENTS

2 aubergines (total weight about 450g/1lb)
60–75ml/4–5 tbsp olive oil
1 large onion, halved and sliced
2–3 garlic cloves, crushed
1 large red or yellow pepper, seeded and cut into thin strips
2 large courgettes, cut into 1cm/½in slices
675g/1½lb ripe tomatoes, peeled, seeded and chopped, or 475ml/16fl oz/2 cups passata
5ml/1 tsp herbes de Provence
salt and ground black pepper

SERVES 6

1 Preheat the grill. Cut the aubergines into 2cm/¾in slices. Brush both sides with olive oil and then grill until lightly browned, turning once. Cut the aubergine slices into cubes and set aside.

2 Heat 15ml/1 tbsp of the remaining oil in a flameproof casserole dish. Cook the onion over a medium heat for about 10 minutes until golden, stirring frequently. Add the garlic, pepper and courgettes. Cook for 10 minutes more.

3 Stir in the tomatoes or passata and aubergine cubes with the dried herbs. Add salt and pepper to taste and simmer gently, covered, for about 20 minutes. Stir the mixture occasionally.

4 Remove the lid and cook for 20 minutes more or until all the vegetables are tender and the cooking liquid has thickened. Tip into a bowl and cool quickly, then pack in a plastic tub. Serve at room temperature with plenty of bread to mop up the delicious juices. Cornets of pepper salami would be good with this picnic salad.

French Bean Salad

INGREDIENTS

175g/6oz cherry tomatoes, halved
5ml/1 tsp granulated sugar
450g/1lb French beans, trimmed
175g/6oz feta cheese, cut in small wedges
salt and ground black pepper
DRESSING
45ml/3 tbsp white wine vinegar
1.5ml/¼ tsp Dijon mustard
2 garlic cloves, crushed
90ml/6 tbsp olive oil

SERVES 6

1 Preheat the oven to 230°C/450°F/Gas 8. Put the cherry tomatoes on a baking sheet with the cut sides up. Sprinkle over the sugar and add salt and pepper to taste. Bake the tomatoes in the preheated oven for about 20 minutes, then leave them to cool.

2 Bring a saucepan of lightly salted water to the boil. Add the French beans and cook for about 10 minutes. Meanwhile, make the dressing. Mix the white wine  vinegar, mustard and garlic in a bowl. Gradually whisk in the oil and add salt and pepper to taste.

3 Drain the cooked beans, tip them into a bowl and immediately pour over the dressing. Toss well to ensure the dressing is evenly distributed.

4 When the beans have cooled, stir in the roasted cherry tomatoes and the wedges of feta cheese. Pack the salad in a sealed plastic tub and keep in the fridge before transporting to the picnic site in a chiller bag.

Potato Salad with Sausage

INGREDIENTS

450g/1lb small waxy potatoes
30–45ml/2–3 tbsp dry white wine
2 shallots, finely chopped
15ml/1 tbsp chopped fresh parsley
15ml/1 tbsp chopped fresh tarragon
175g/6oz cooked garlic sausage,
such as kielbasa, sliced
parsley sprig, to garnish
DRESSING
15ml/1 tbsp tarragon vinegar
10ml/2 tsp Dijon mustard
75ml/5 tbsp olive oil
salt and ground black pepper

SERVES 4

1 Put the potatoes in a saucepan with lightly salted cold water to cover. Bring to the boil, lower the heat and simmer for 10–15 minutes until they are tender.

2 Drain the potatoes, refresh them under cold running water and drain again. Peel the potatoes if you prefer, or leave in their skins. Cut into 5mm/¼in slices, place in a bowl and sprinkle with the wine and shallots.

3 Make the dressing. Mix the vinegar and mustard in a bowl. Gradually whisk in the oil, and season to taste. Pour the dressing over the potato mixture.

4 Then sprinkle the chopped parsley and tarragon over the salad, and add the sausage slices. Toss lightly to mix. Season with salt and pepper. Pack in a plastic tub and serve at room temperature, garnished with a fresh parsley sprig.

VARIATION

If preferred, leave out the sausage and serve the potato salad as it is, with rollmop herrings.

Frisée Salad with Bacon

INGREDIENTS

1 frisée lettuce, separated into leaves
45ml/3 tbsp extra-virgin olive oil
175g/6oz piece of smoked bacon, diced
1 thick slice of white bread, crust removed, diced
DRESSING
1 garlic clove, bruised
15ml/1 tbsp red wine vinegar
10ml/2 tsp Dijon mustard
45ml/3 tbsp olive oil
salt and ground black pepper

SERVES 4

1 Tear the lettuce leaves into bite-size pieces and place in a bowl. Wash, dry and store in a plastic bag in the salad compartment of the fridge.

2 Heat 15ml/1 tbsp of the oil in a frying pan. Add the bacon and fry over a medium heat until well browned, stirring occasionally. Using a slotted spoon, lift out the bacon pieces and drain on kitchen paper.

3 Add a further 30ml/2 tbsp oil to the pan. When hot, fry the bread cubes, turning frequently, until evenly browned. Remove the croûtons with a slotted spoon and drain them on kitchen paper. When cold, pack the croûtons and bacon in separate plastic tubs.

4 Make the dressing. Mix the garlic, vinegar, mustard and oil in a leakproof beaker. Season with salt and pepper to taste.

5 Pack the lettuce, bacon, croûtons and dressing separately. When ready to serve, tip the lettuce into a salad bowl and add the bacon and croûtons. Shake the dressing well and pour it over the salad. Toss quickly, making sure the salad leaves are evenly covered, and serve.

COOK'S TIP

For serving at home, make this a warm salad. Fry the croûtons first, then the bacon cubes. Drain them on kitchen paper. Add the garlic, vinegar, mustard and remaining oil to the frying pan. Whisk over the heat until warm, then pour over the lettuce and toss lightly. To serve, sprinkle the lettuce with the fried bacon and croûtons.

Spanish Potatoes

INGREDIENTS

675g / 1½lb small new potatoes
2 garlic cloves, sliced
1 small dried red chilli, crumbled
2.5ml / ½ tsp ground cumin
10ml / 2 tsp mild paprika
30ml / 2 tbsp red wine vinegar
75ml / 5 tbsp olive oil
1 red or green pepper, seeded and sliced
coarse sea salt to serve

SERVES 4

1 Put the potatoes in a saucepan with lightly salted cold water to cover. Bring to the boil, lower the heat and simmer for 15 minutes until they are tender.

2 Drain the potatoes, refresh them under cold running water and drain again. Peel the potatoes if you prefer, or leave in their skins. Cut into chunks.

3 Put the sliced garlic and chilli in a mortar. Crush with a pestle, then add the ground cumin, paprika and red wine vinegar and mix to form a paste.

4 Heat the oil in a large frying pan and fry the potatoes until golden, turning them often. Add the pepper slices and cook for 1 minute, then stir in the garlic paste. Cook, stirring, for 2 minutes. Tip the spiced potatoes into a bowl and leave to cool. Cover the bowl securely for packing and grind sea salt over the potatoes just before serving.

Swiss Cheese Salad

INGREDIENTS

2 skinless, boneless chicken breasts
300ml/½ pint/1¼ cups chicken stock
225g/8oz Gruyere cheese
225g/8oz thickly sliced cooked ham
or ox tongue
1 lollo rosso lettuce
1 butterhead lettuce
1 bunch watercress
3 celery sticks, sliced
60ml/4 tbsp sesame seeds, toasted
2 green-skinned eating apples
DRESSING
75ml/5 tbsp sunflower oil
5ml/1 tsp sesame oil
45ml/3 tbsp lemon juice
10ml/2 tsp chopped fresh mint
3 drops of Tabasco sauce

SERVES 4

1 Put the chicken breasts in a saucepan. Pour over the stock and bring to simmering point. Simmer for 15 minutes or until the chicken is just cooked. Drain, reserving the stock for another recipe. Cool the chicken quickly.

2 Make the dressing by mixing all the ingredients in a leakproof beaker. Cut the chicken, cheese and ham or tongue into fine strips. Put in a tub, moisten with a little of the dressing and chill in the fridge until required.

3 Wash and dry the salad leaves. Pack them, with the celery, in a loosely-closed plastic bag in a chiller box. Add the tub of cheese and cold meat strips and pack the sesame seeds and apples separately, with the dressing. Dress the leaves and assemble the salad on individual plates at the picnic site, slicing the apple and adding it at the last minute.

Stuffed Peppers

INGREDIENTS

6 even-size peppers, any colour
60ml/4 tbsp olive oil, plus extra for drizzling
1 large onion, finely chopped
3 drained canned anchovy fillets, chopped
2 garlic cloves, crushed
3 tomatoes, peeled and diced
60ml/4 tbsp white wine
450g/1lb/4 cups cooked rice (about
200g/7oz/1 cup raw weight)
45ml/3 tbsp finely chopped fresh parsley
115g/4oz/⅔ cup diced mozzarella cheese
90ml/6 tbsp grated Parmesan cheese
salt and ground black pepper
flat-leaf parsley, to garnish

SERVES 6

1 Preheat the oven to 190°C/375°F/Gas 5. Cut the tops off the peppers and remove the cores and seeds. Trim the bottoms, if necessary, so that they stand level. Bring a saucepan of lightly salted water to the boil, add the peppers and blanch for 3–4 minutes. Lift out with a slotted spoon and dry inside and out with kitchen paper.

2 Heat the olive oil in a large frying pan and fry the chopped onion for about 5 minutes, until softened. Stir in the chopped anchovy fillets, garlic, tomatoes and white wine. Cook, stirring occasionally, for 5 minutes.

3 Off the heat, stir the cooked rice, fresh parsley, mozzarella and two-thirds of the Parmesan into the onion mixture. Season with salt and pepper to taste. Sprinkle the pepper cavities with salt and pepper, then stuff with the filling.

4 Stand the peppers upright in a shallow baking dish that will just hold them comfortably. Top with the remaining Parmesan and drizzle with a little olive oil. Pour in enough water to come 1cm/½in up the sides of the peppers.

5 Bake the peppers in the preheated oven for about 25 minutes, then allow them to cool to room temperature. Transport the peppers to the picnic site in the dish in which they were baked, using balls of crumpled foil to keep them upright. Garnish each of the peppers with a sprig of flat-leaf parsley before serving.

Main Attractions

Chicken & Apricot Filo Pie

INGREDIENTS

75g/3oz/½ cup bulgur wheat
120ml/4fl oz/½ cup boiling water
75g/3oz/6 tbsp butter
1 onion, chopped
450g/1lb/2 cups minced chicken
50g/2oz/¼ cup ready-to-eat dried apricots,
finely chopped
25g/1oz/¼ cup blanched almonds, chopped
5ml/1 tsp ground cinnamon
2.5ml/½ tsp ground allspice
60ml/4 tbsp Greek yogurt
15ml/1 tbsp snipped fresh chives
30ml/2 tbsp chopped fresh parsley
6 large sheets of filo pastry
salt and ground black pepper, to taste
halved fresh chives, to garnish

SERVES 6

1 Preheat the oven to 200°C/400°F/Gas 6. Soak the bulgur wheat in boiling water for 10 minutes, until the water is absorbed. Drain and squeeze dry.

2 Heat 25g/1oz/2 tbsp of the butter in a frying pan. Fry the onion and chicken gently until golden. Stir in the apricots, almonds and bulgur wheat; cook for 2 minutes more. Off the heat, stir in the spices, yogurt, fresh herbs and seasoning.

3 Melt the remaining butter. Cut the filo into 25cm/10in rounds. Layer three rounds in a 23cm/9in loose-based flan tin, brushing each of the layers with melted butter. Spoon in the chicken mixture, then crumple the remaining filo rounds, brush each one with butter, and place them on top of the pie.

4 Brush over any remaining butter and bake for about 30 minutes, until the crust is golden and crisp. When the tin has cooled, pack it carefully in a rigid box (filo is fragile). Serve the pie in wedges, garnished with fresh chives.

Stuffed Turkey Breast with Lemon

INGREDIENTS

675g/1½lb turkey breast, in one piece
1 carrot, cut into matchsticks
1 courgette, cut into matchsticks
75g/3oz cooked ham, cut into matchsticks
2 thick slices of white bread, crusts removed,
soaked in a little milk to soften
10 stoned green olives, finely chopped
1 large garlic clove, crushed
60ml/4 tbsp chopped fresh parsley
60ml/4 tbsp finely shredded fresh basil
1 egg, lightly beaten
1.5ml/¼ tsp grated lemon rind
30ml/2 tbsp grated Parmesan cheese
60ml/4 tbsp olive oil
250ml/8fl oz/1 cup warm chicken stock
½ lemon, cut in thin wedges
salt and ground black pepper

SERVES 4–5

1 Remove any bones, skin or fat from the turkey. Cut part of the way through the breast so that the halves can be opened out like a book. Pound the meat to obtain one large piece of even thickness.

2 Preheat the oven to 200°C/400°F/Gas 6. Blanch the carrot and courgette sticks in a pan of boiling water for 2 minutes. Then drain and mix with the ham.

3 Squeeze the bread dry, place it in a mixing bowl and break it up with a fork. Add the olives, garlic, herbs, egg, lemon rind and Parmesan cheese. Season with salt and pepper and mix well.

4 Then spread the bread mixture over the meat, leaving a narrow border around the outside. Arrange the vegetable and ham matchsticks on top, then roll the turkey up and tie it with a piece of string.

5 Heat the olive oil in a flameproof casserole dish and brown the turkey roll. Add the stock and lemon wedges, cover the dish and bake in the oven for 15 minutes. Remove the lid and the lemon wedges. Bake, uncovered, for 30 minutes more until the roll is fully cooked, basting occasionally. Cool quickly. Wrap the turkey roll in double foil and slice at the picnic site. Serve solo with green salad or with a lemon mayonnaise.

Cod Plaki

INGREDIENTS

300ml/½ pint/1¼ cups olive oil
2 onions, thinly sliced
3 beefsteak tomatoes, roughly chopped
3 garlic cloves, thinly sliced
5ml/1 tsp granulated sugar
5ml/1 tsp chopped fresh dill
5ml/1 tsp chopped fresh mint
5ml/1 tsp chopped fresh celery leaves
15ml/1 tbsp chopped fresh parsley
300ml/½ pint/1¼ cups water
6 cod steaks
juice of 1 lemon
salt and ground black pepper
fresh herbs, to garnish

SERVES 6

2 Place the fish steaks on top of the mixture and cook gently for 10–12 minutes or until the fish is just cooked. Pour over the lemon juice. Lift out the

cod steaks with a slotted spoon and arrange them in a picnic dish. Spoon the sauce over and cool quickly. Cover the dish tightly and pack in a chiller bag. Garnish with fresh herbs to serve.

1 Heat the oil in a frying pan and fry the onions until golden. Add the tomatoes, garlic, sugar and chopped herbs Cook for 2 minutes more, then pour over the

water. Add seasoning and simmer for 25 minutes or until the liquid has reduced by one-third.

Sweet Potato Roulade

INGREDIENTS

450g/1lb sweet potatoes, freshly boiled
12 allspice berries, crushed
4 eggs, separated
50g/2oz/½ cup grated Edam or
Cheddar cheese
salt and ground black pepper
15ml/1 tbsp sesame seeds
FILLING
225g/8oz/1 cup low-fat soft cheese
75ml/5 tbsp natural yogurt
6–8 spring onions, thinly sliced
30ml/2 tbsp chopped Brazil nuts, roasted

SERVES 6

3 Whisk the egg whites to stiff peaks. Lightly stir one-third of the whites into the sweet potato mixture to lighten it, then fold in the rest. Spoon the mixture into the prepared tin, level the surface and bake for 10–15 minutes until firm to the touch.

4 Have ready a sheet of non-stick baking paper on a clean dish towel. Sprinkle the paper with the sesame seeds, then carefully invert the cooked sponge on to it. Trim the edges, roll the sponge up and leave to cool. Unroll, spread with the filling and roll up again. Pack in a rigid box and slice at the picnic site. Serve with salad leaves.

103

1 Preheat the oven to 200°C/400°F/Gas 6. Grease a 33 x 25cm/13 x 10in Swiss roll tin and line with non-stick baking paper. Make the filling by mixing the soft cheese, yogurt, spring onions and nuts in a bowl. Cover the mixture and keep in the fridge until required.

2 Chop the sweet potato roughly and put it in a food processor with the allspice. Pulse until just smooth, then spoon into a bowl and stir in the egg yolks and cheese, with salt and pepper to taste.

Mediterranean Quiche

INGREDIENTS

225g/8oz/2 cups plain flour
pinch of salt
pinch of mustard powder
115g/4oz/½ cup chilled butter, cubed
50g/2oz/½ cup grated Gruyère cheese
30ml/2 tbsp mild French mustard
FILLING
50g/2oz can anchovies, drained
60ml/4 tbsp milk
45ml/3 tbsp olive oil
2 large Spanish onions, sliced
1 red pepper, seeded and sliced
3 egg yolks
350ml/12fl oz/1½ cups double cream
1 garlic clove, crushed
*175g/6oz/1½ cups grated mature
Cheddar cheese*
2 large tomatoes, thickly sliced
salt and ground black pepper
shredded fresh basil, to garnish

SERVES 10–12

1 Mix the flour, salt and mustard powder in a food processor. Add the butter and pulse the mixture until it resembles breadcrumbs. Add the cheese and process briefly. With the motor running, add iced water until the mixture forms a ball. Wrap the dough in clear film and chill for 30 minutes.

2 Preheat the oven to 200°C/400°F/Gas 6. Make the filling. Soak the anchovies in the milk for 20 minutes. Heat the oil in a frying pan and fry the onions and red pepper until soft. In a bowl, beat the egg yolks, cream, garlic and Cheddar cheese with plenty of salt and pepper.

3 Roll out the pastry on a lightly floured surface and line a 23cm/9in loose-based flan tin. Spread the mustard over the pastry case. Arrange the toma-  toes in a layer on the bottom, add the onion mixture, and drain and arrange the anchovies on top.

4 Pour over the egg mixture and bake for 20–25 minutes. Lower the oven temperature to 180°C/350°F/Gas 4 and bake for 25 minutes more. Cool, wrap the tin in foil and pack it in a rigid box. Serve the quiche in slices, garnished with the fresh basil.

104

Broccoli & Chestnut Terrine

INGREDIENTS

450g / 1lb broccoli, cut into small florets
225g / 8oz cooked chestnuts, roughly chopped
50g / 2oz / 1 cup fresh wholemeal breadcrumbs
60ml / 4 tbsp natural yogurt
30ml / 2 tbsp grated Parmesan cheese
2 eggs, beaten
salt and ground black pepper

SERVES 4–6

106

1 Preheat the oven to 180°C/350°F/Gas 4. Line a 900g/2lb loaf tin with non-stick baking paper. Blanch or steam the broccoli for 3–4 minutes until just tender. Drain well. Set aside about a quarter of the smallest florets and chop the rest finely.

2 In a large bowl, mix the chopped chestnuts, breadcrumbs, natural yogurt and Parmesan cheese. Stir in salt and pepper to taste, then fold in the chopped broccoli florets and beaten eggs.

3 Gently fold the reserved florets into the mixture. Spoon into the prepared loaf tin and level the surface with the back of a wooden spoon.

4 Place the tin in a roasting pan and pour in boiling water to come halfway up the sides of the tin. Bake for 25 minutes. Cool quickly, wrap the tin in foil and pack it in a box. At the picnic site, turn it out on to a board. Cut into slices and serve with salad leaves and cold new potatoes, if liked.

COOK'S TIP
For an unbeatable taste sensation, serve the terrine with Spanish Potatoes and fresh cherry tomatoes.

Country Pie

INGREDIENTS

900g / 2lb puff pastry, thawed if frozen
beaten egg, to glaze
FILLING
1 small duck
1 small chicken
350g / 12oz pork belly, minced
1 egg, lightly beaten
2 shallots, finely chopped
2.5ml / ½ tsp ground cinnamon
2.5ml / ½ tsp grated nutmeg
5ml / 1 tsp Worcestershire sauce
finely grated rind of 1 lemon
salt and ground black pepper
175ml / 6fl oz / ¾ cup red wine
600ml / 1 pint / 2½ cups well-flavoured stock
15g / ½ oz / 1 tbsp gelatine
HOT WATER PASTRY
675g / 1½lb / 6 cups plain flour
225g / 8 oz hard white fat, cubed
300ml / ½ pint / 1¼ cups water
beaten egg, to glaze

SERVES 12

108

1 Make the filling. Dice the poultry breasts and set them aside. Trim the carcasses, and mix the meat with the pork. Add the beaten egg, shallots, spices, Worcestershire sauce and lemon rind. Season well. Pour over all but 15ml / 1 tbsp of wine. Marinate for 15 minutes.

2 Make the pastry. Sift the flour into a bowl. Bring the fat and water to the boil, pour it on to the flour and mix quickly to a dough. Cool slightly, then knead. Keep warm, covered with a cloth.

3 Preheat the oven to 200°C/400°F/Gas 6. Roll out the pastry on a lightly floured surface. Use two-thirds of the pastry to line a greased 25cm/10in cake tin; allow a little pastry to hang over the top. Fill with alternate layers of pork mixture and diced poultry and ham. Make a lid with the remaining pastry and seal well. Cut two large holes in the lid and add pastry decorations.

4 Bake for 20 minutes, glaze with egg and lower the oven temperature to 180°C/350°F/Gas 4. Cover the pie with foil and bake for 1 hour more.

5 Degrease the stock. Pour the stock into a pan, heat and whisk in the gelatine until no lumps are left. Insert a funnel in the pie and pour in the stock. Chill the pie in the fridge for 24 hours, before wrapping and packing. Cut the pie into thick wedges to serve.

Wild Mushroom Pie

INGREDIENTS

450g/1lb puff pastry, thawed if frozen
beaten egg, to glaze
FILLING
150g/5oz/²/3 cup butter
2 shallots, finely chopped
2 garlic cloves, crushed
450g/1lb/4 cups mixed wild mushrooms,
sliced
45ml/3 tbsp chopped fresh parsley
30ml/2 tbsp double cream
salt and ground black pepper

SERVES 6

1 Make the filling. Melt 50g/2oz/¼ cup of the butter in a large saucepan. Gently fry the chopped shallots and crushed garlic cloves over a low heat for about 5 minutes, until softened but not browned.

2 Then add the remaining butter to the pan. When it has melted, stir in the mushrooms and cook over a low heat for 35–40 minutes. Pour off the excess liquid and stir in the chopped parsley and double cream, adding salt and ground black pepper to taste. Allow the mixture to cool.

3 Preheat the oven to 220°C/425°F/Gas 7. Roll out half the pastry on a lightly floured surface. Using a plate as a guide, cut out a 23cm/9in round. Place the round on a baking sheet and pile the filling in the centre. Roll out the rest of the pastry and cut a slightly larger round, to cover the base and filling. Lop the pastry over the rolling pin and lay it over the filling, then firmly press the pastry edges together to seal.

4 Brush the top of the pie with beaten egg to glaze and decorate with pastry trimmings. Cut three holes in the top of the crust. Bake in the oven for 45 minutes or until the pastry has risen and is golden. Turn out the pie on to a wire rack and allow to cool completely, then wrap the pie in foil and transport to the picnic site in a rigid box. Cut the pie into thick wedges to serve.

Sweet Treats

Apple Crumble Cake

INGREDIENTS

CRUMBLE TOPPING
75g / 3oz / ³⁄4 cup self-raising flour
2.5ml / ½ tsp ground cinnamon
40g / 1½oz / 3 tbsp butter
25g / 1oz / 2 tbsp caster sugar
FRUIT BASE
50g / 2oz / 4 tbsp butter, softened
75g / 3oz / 6 tbsp caster sugar
1 size 3 egg, beaten
115g / 4oz / 1 cup self-raising flour, sifted
2 cooking apples, peeled, cored and sliced
50g / 2oz / ⅓ cup sultanas

SERVES 8–10

1 Preheat the oven to 180°C/350°F/Gas 4. Grease a deep 18cm/7 inch springform tin, line the base with greaseproof paper and grease the paper.

2 Make the topping. Sift the flour and cinnamon into a large mixing bowl. Rub the butter into the flour until it resembles breadcrumbs, then stir in the sugar. Set aside.

3 Make the fruit base. Place the butter, sugar, egg and flour in a bowl and beat for 1–2 minutes until smooth. Spoon into the prepared tin.

4 Mix together the apple slices and sultanas and spread them evenly over the top. Sprinkle with the topping. Bake in the centre of the oven for about 1 hour. Cool in the tin for 10 minutes before turning out on to a wire rack and peeling off the lining paper.

5 Decorate the cake with slices of red dessert apple and sprinkle with caster sugar and a pinch of ground cinnamon. Transport the cake to the picnic in a tin. Serve in thick slices with cream, if liked.

113

Savarin with Summer Fruit

INGREDIENTS

115g/4oz/½ cup butter, softened
275g/10oz/2½ cups plain flour
10g/¼oz sachet easy-blend dried yeast
60ml/4 tbsp caster sugar
4 eggs, beaten
60ml/4 tbsp hand-hot water
5ml/1 tsp vanilla essence
450g/1lb fresh raspberries or
strawberries, hulled
mint leaves, to decorate
clotted cream, to serve
SYRUP
225g/8oz/1 cup caster sugar
600ml/1 pint/2½ cups water
90ml/6 tbsp redcurrant jelly
45ml/3 tbsp Kirsch (optional)

SERVES 4–6

1 Using 15ml/1 tbsp of the butter, generously grease a 23cm/9in ring mould. Put the flour, yeast and sugar in a food processor and pulse to mix. With the motor running, add the beaten eggs, water and vanilla essence through the feeder tube. Process to a soft dough, scraping down the sides of the processor as needed, then add the remaining butter and pulse about 10 times to incorporate it.

2 Place the dough in evenly spaced spoonfuls around the ring mould. Cover the mould and leave the dough to rise until it has doubled in bulk. Preheat the oven to 200°C/400°F/Gas 6.

3 Place the ring mould in the oven and immediately turn the heat down to 180°C/350°F/Gas 4. Bake for 25 minutes until golden brown and springy to the touch. Cool on a wire rack.

4 Make the syrup by heating the sugar, water and two-thirds of the redcurrant jelly in a pan. Stir until smooth, then boil for 3 minutes. Cool slightly, then add the Kirsch, if using. Stir 30ml/2 tbsp of the syrup into the reserved redcurrant jelly until dissolved, to make a glaze. Set aside.

5 Place the warm cake on a wire rack over a baking tray. Spoon the syrup over repeatedly until absorbed, then carefully place the cake in a shallow serving dish and pour over any remaining syrup. Brush the redcurrant glaze over the top. Cover and transport very carefully. Pack the berries, cream and mint leaves separately. At the picnic, fill the centre with berries. Decorate, then serve with cream.

114

Raspberry Crumble Muffins

INGREDIENTS

175g/6oz/1½ cups plain flour
10ml/2 tsp baking powder
pinch of salt
50g/2oz/¼ cup caster sugar
50g/2oz/¼ cup soft light brown sugar
5ml/1 tsp ground cinnamon
115g/4oz/½ cup butter, melted
1 egg, beaten
120ml/4fl oz/½ cup milk
150g/5oz/scant 1 cup raspberries
grated rind of 1 lemon
CRUMBLE TOPPING
25g/1oz/3 tbsp pecan nuts or walnuts,
finely chopped
50g/2oz/¼ cup soft dark brown sugar
45ml/3 tbsp plain flour
5ml/1 tsp ground cinnamon
40g/1½oz/3 tbsp butter, melted

MAKES 12

1 Preheat the oven to 180°C/350°F/Gas 4. Lightly grease a 12-cup muffin tin, or use paper cases. Sift the flour, baking powder and salt into a bowl. Stir in the sugars and cinnamon.

2 Make a well in the centre. Add the butter, egg and milk and mix until just combined. Stir in the raspberries and lemon rind. Divide the mixture among the muffin cups.

3 Make the crumble topping by mixing the nuts, dark brown sugar, flour and cinnamon in a bowl. Add the melted butter and stir to blend. Spoon some of the crumble over each uncooked muffin. Bake in the oven for 20–25 minutes, or until the muffins are well risen and golden brown. Allow to cool on a wire rack, then pack in a tin.

Dried Fruit Tea Bread

INGREDIENTS

170g/6oz/1 cup dried fruit, roughly chopped
250 ml/8fl oz/1 cup hot tea
225g/8oz/2 cups wholemeal self-raising
flour
5ml/1 tsp grated nutmeg
50g/2oz/¼ cup dark muscovado sugar
45ml/3 tbsp sunflower oil
45ml/3 tbsp skimmed milk
demerara sugar, for sprinkling

SERVES 8–10

1 Soak the chopped dried fruit in the hot tea for several hours or overnight, making sure the fruit is completely covered. Drain and reserve both the fruit and the liquid.

2 Preheat the oven to 180°C/350°F/Gas 4. Grease a 7in/18cm round cake tin and line the base with non-stick baking paper. Take care to grease the paper well.

3 Sift the flour into a large bowl with the grated nutmeg. Stir in the muscovado sugar, fruit and tea. Add the sunflower oil and skimmed milk and mix well.

4 Spoon the mixture into the prepared tin and sprinkle with demerara sugar. Bake for 50–55 minutes or until the mixture is just firm. Cool on a wire rack then cut into thick chunks and pack in a tin.

Biscotti

INGREDIENTS

50g/2oz/¼ cup unsalted butter, softened
115g/4oz/½ cup caster sugar
175g/6oz/1½ cups self-raising flour
1.5ml/¼ tsp salt
10ml/2 tsp baking powder
5ml/1 tsp ground coriander
finely grated rind of 1 lemon
50g/2oz/¼ cup polenta
1 egg, lightly beaten
10ml/2 tsp brandy or orange liqueur
50g/2oz/¼ cup pistachio nuts

MAKES 24

1 Preheat the oven to 160°C/325°F/Gas 3. Lightly grease a baking sheet. In a mixing bowl, cream the butter with the sugar until the mixture is light and fluffy.

2 Sift the flour, salt, baking powder and coriander into the mixing bowl. Add the lemon rind, polenta, egg and brandy or liqueur. Mix to a soft dough.

3 Work in the nuts until they are evenly distributed. Halve the mixture and then shape each half into a long sausage, about 23cm/9in long and 6cm/  2½in wide. Place on the baking sheet and bake for about 30 minutes until risen and just firm. Remove the baking sheet, but leave the oven on.

4 When the loaves are cool, use a serrated knife to cut each of them diagonally into 12 thin slices. Place the slices on the baking sheet, cut-side up, and bake for 10 minutes more, until crisp. Cool on a wire rack, then pack in a tin.

COOK'S TIP
These Italian biscuits are traditionally served dipped in a sweet dessert wine – ideal for those who don't have to drive home from the picnic.

Figs with Ricotta Cream

INGREDIENTS

115g/4oz/½ cup ricotta cheese
45ml/3 tbsp crème fraîche
15ml/1 tbsp clear honey
2.5ml/½ tsp vanilla essence
4 ripe, fresh figs
grated nutmeg, to decorate

SERVES 4

1 Mix the ricotta cheese, crème fraîche, honey and vanilla essence in a bowl. Transfer to a tub with a tight-fitting lid and pack in a chiller bag with the figs.

Pack a nutmeg – and a nutmeg grater – if you really want to impress.

2 When ready to serve, trim the stalks from the figs. Make four cuts through each fig from the stalk end, cutting them almost through, but leaving them joined at the base. Place each fig on an individual plate and open it out like a flower.

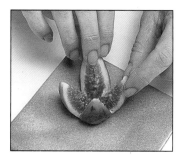

3 Spoon a little ricotta cream on to each plate and grate nutmeg on top to serve.

VARIATION

Use low-fat cream cheese instead of ricotta, if you prefer, and substitute Greek yogurt for the crème fraîche. Sprinkle the yogurt with demerara sugar.

Chocolate Chip Banana Crêpes

INGREDIENTS

2 ripe bananas
200ml / 7fl oz / scant 1 cup milk
2 eggs
150g / 5oz / 1¼ cups self-raising flour
40g / 1½oz / ⅓ cup ground almonds
15ml / 1 tbsp caster sugar
45ml / 3 tbsp plain chocolate chips
butter for frying
TOPPING
150ml / ¼ pint / ⅔ cup double cream
15ml / 1 tbsp icing sugar
toasted flaked almonds

MAKES 16

1 Mash the bananas in a bowl with a fork. Stir in half the milk, then beat in the eggs. Gradually beat in the flour, ground almonds and caster sugar. Make a well in the centre of the mixture and pour in the remaining milk. Add the chocolate chips and stir to make a thick batter.

2 Heat a knob of butter in a non-stick frying pan. Spoon in a little of the batter, so that it spreads to form a small crêpe. Make more crêpes in the same way, but do not overcrowd the pan.

3 When bubbles appear on the top of the crêpes, turn them over and briefly cook the other side. Cool on a wire rack, then pack into a tin.

4 For the topping, either whip the cream with the icing sugar and pack in a sealed tub in a chiller bag, or cheat and use aerosol cream. Pack the toasted flaked almonds separately, to decorate the crêpes.

COOK'S TIP

The easiest way to cook these is in an electric frying pan, if you have one. Children enjoy making them (with adult help), especially if they are allowed to use the chocolate chips to make faces on the crêpes.

121

Orange-blossom Jelly

INGREDIENTS

75ml/5 tbsp caster sugar
150ml/¼ pint/⅔ cup water
30ml/2 tbsp powdered gelatine
*600ml/1 pint/2½ cups freshly squeezed
orange juice*
30ml/2 tbsp orange-flower water

SERVES 4–6

1 Place the caster sugar and water in a small saucepan. Heat gently, stirring occasionally, until the sugar has dissolved. Tip into a heatproof bowl and sprinkle

in the gelatine. Leave to stand until the gelatine has absorbed the liquid and is solid.

2 Melt the gelatine again, by placing the bowl over a pan of gently simmering water. When it is clear, remove it from the heat. Leave the gelatine to cool, but do not let it solidify. Stir it into the orange juice and add the orange-flower water.

3 Then wet a jelly mould, pour in the orange jelly and chill in the fridge for at least 3 hours until solidly set. Turn the jelly out by immersing the mould in a bowl

of hot water. Return the jelly to the mould and wrap it carefully in a chiller bag to transport to the picnic. Turn the jelly out to serve; for a special occasion, decorate with fresh flowers. Serve with dessert biscuits such as langues de chat, if you like.

COOK'S TIP

*The acid in orange juice inhibits the setting
action of gelatine, which is why the quantity in
this recipe is relatively high. It is important to
cool the liquid gelatine before adding it to the
orange juice, or it will form threads.*

122

Lemon Tart

INGREDIENTS

*350g/12oz shortcrust or sweet
shortcrust pastry
grated rind of 2 large lemons
150ml/¼ pint/⅔ cup freshly squeezed
lemon juice
115g/4oz/½ cup caster sugar
60ml/4 tbsp crème fraîche or double cream
4 eggs, plus 3 egg yolks
icing sugar, for dusting*

SERVES 8–10

1 Preheat the oven to 190°C/375°F/ Gas 5. Roll out the pastry on a lightly floured surface and line a 23cm/9in flan tin. Prick the base of the pastry, line with foil and baking beans and bake blind for 15 minutes. Remove the foil and beans and return the pastry case to the oven to cook for a further 5–7 minutes, until golden.

2 Whisk the lemon rind, juice and sugar in a bowl until light and fluffy. Gradually whisk in the crème fraîche or double cream, then add the whole eggs one at a time, whisking after each addition. Then whisk in the egg yolks.

3 Pour the filling into the pastry case and bake in the oven for 15–20 minutes, until set. Leave to cool and then pack the tart, still supported by the tin, in a rigid box. Transfer the tart to a plate at the picnic site and dust with icing sugar to serve.

Pear & Almond Cream Tart

INGREDIENTS

*350g / 12oz shortcrust or sweet
shortcrust pastry
3 firm pears
lemon juice
15ml / 1 tbsp peach brandy or water
60ml / 4 tbsp peach preserve, strained*
ALMOND CREAM FILLING
*65g / 2½oz / 5 tbsp butter
60ml / 4 tbsp caster sugar
75g / 3oz / ¾ cup ground almonds
1 egg, plus 1 egg white
few drops of almond essence*

SERVES 6

1 Preheat the oven to 190°C/375°F/Gas 5. Roll out the pastry on a lightly floured surface and line a 23cm/9in flan tin. Make the almond cream filling by creaming the butter with the sugar in a small bowl, then stirring in the ground almonds, egg, egg white and almond essence.

2 Peel the pears, cut them in half and remove the cores. Brush with lemon juice to stop them from going brown. With the rounded sides up, slice the pears thinly crossways, keeping the slices together.

3 Spoon the almond cream filling into the uncooked pastry case. Slide a palette knife under each pear in turn, gently pressing the top to fan out the slices, and transfer it to the pastry case. Arrange the pears like the spokes of a wheel. Bake the tart in the oven for 50–55 minutes or until the filling is set and golden brown. Cool on a wire rack.

4 Meanwhile, heat the brandy or water with the peach preserve in a small pan, then brush the mixture over the top of the hot tart to glaze. Leave until quite cold, then wrap carefully and transport to the picnic in a rigid box.

125

Peach Leaf Pie

INGREDIENTS

1.2kg/2½lb ripe peaches, peeled and sliced
juice of 1 lemon
90g/3½oz/½ cup caster sugar
45ml/3 tbsp cornflour
1.5ml/¼ tsp grated nutmeg
2.5ml/½ tsp ground cinnamon
1 egg beaten with 1 tbsp water, to glaze
25g/1oz/2 tbsp butter, diced
cream, to serve
PASTRY
225g/8oz/2 cups plain flour
2.5ml/¾ tsp salt
150g/5oz/⅔ cup cold butter, cut in pieces
75-90ml/5-6 tbsp iced water

SERVES 8

1 Sift the flour and salt into a bowl. Rub in the butter, then stir in just enough iced water to bind the dough. Gather into two balls, one slightly larger than the other. Wrap and chill for at least 20 minutes. Preheat the oven to 220°C/425°F/Gas 7.

2 Combine the peaches with the lemon juice, sugar, cornflour and spices. Set aside.

3 Roll out the larger dough ball thinly and line a 23cm/9in pie dish. Roll out the remaining dough. Cut out 7.5cm/3in leaves. Mark with veins.

4 Brush the bottom of the pie shell with egg glaze. Add the peaches, piling them higher in the centre. Dot with the butter. Starting from the rim of the dish,  cover the peaches with concentric rings of leaves. Place tiny balls of dough in the centre, if you like. Brush with the glaze. Bake for 10 minutes. Lower the heat to 180°C/350°F/Gas 4 and bake for 35–40 minutes more. Serve cold with cream.

Index

Apple: char-grilled, 58
  crumble cake, 113
Aubergine & feta rolls, 50

Bacon kofta kebabs, 20
Bananas, baked, 60
Beans: red bean & mushroom
  burgers, 48
Beef, 10
  peppered steak, 18
  Tex-Mex burgers, 16
Biscotti, 118
Blue cheese dressing, 72
Breads, 70
Brie parcels, 51
Broccoli & chestnut terrine, 106
Bulgur salad, 20

Cakes and bakes, 70
Calamari, barbecued stuffed, 41
Cheese: aubergine & feta rolls,
  50
  blue cheese dressing, 72
  brie parcels, 51
  cheese & chive scones, 84
  Swiss cheese salad, 95
Chicken, 10
  blackened Cajun chicken &
    corn, 30
  chicken & apricot filo pie, 99
  chicken & citrus kebabs, 27

chicken with herb & ricotta
  stuffing, 35
  country pie, 108
  crudités, 70
  Deep South salad, 28
  spiced chicken breasts, 34
Chocolate chip banana crêpes,
  121
Cinnamon toasts, 58
Cod plaki, 102
Country pie, 108
Crêpes, chocolate chip banana,
  121
Croissants, strawberry, 64
Crudités, 70

Deep South salad, 28
Desserts, 70
Dressings, 70, 72
Drinks, 70
Duck: country pie, 108

Falafel, 75
Fennel & lavender tarts, 77

Figs with ricotta cream, 120
Fish, 10, 12,
  char-grilled tuna, 37
  Mexican barbecued salmon,
    38
  grilled sardines with herb salsa,
    42
  Thai spiced fish, 43
Five-spice ribs, 15
French bean salad, 89
French dressing, 72
Frisée salad with bacon, 92
Fruit, 10, 70
  fruit kebabs, 65

Garlic croûtons, 72

Hummus with tahini, 80

Kebabs: bacon kofta kebabs, 20
  chicken & citrus kebabs, 27
  fruit kebabs, 65
  mixed grill skewers, 22
  pork & pineapple satay, 24
  potato skewers, 47
  sweet & sour kebabs, 32

Lamb, 10
  racks of lamb with lavender
    marinade, 19
Lemon tart, 124

Index

Marinating, 13
Mediterranean quiche, 104
Mediterranean vegetables, 52
Mexican barbecued salmon, 38
Mixed grill skewers, 22
Muffins, raspberry crumble, 116
Mushrooms: red bean &
    mushroom burgers, 48
  wild mushroom pie, 110

Nectarines with marzipan &
    mascarpone, 61

Orange-blossom jelly, 122
Oranges in Cointreau & maple
    syrup, 62

Pan bagna, 76
Pastries, 71
Pâtés, 71
Peach leaf pie, 126
Pear & almond cream tart, 125
Peppered steak in beer & garlic,
    18
Peppers, stuffed, 96
Picnic checklist, 71
Pineapple wedges, 57
Pizzas, 71
Polenta, grilled herb, 54
Pork, 11

five-spice ribs, 15
  pork & leek pâté, 78
  pork & pineapple satay, 24
Potatoes: dill & potato cakes, 85
  potato & onion tortilla, 81
  potato salad with sausage, 90
  potato skewers, 47
  Spanish potatoes, 94
Prawns, with walnut pesto, 40

Quiche, Mediterranean, 104

Raspberry crumble muffins, 116
Ratatouille, 88

Salads, 28
  Deep South salad, 28
  French bean salad, 89
  Frisée salad with bacon, 92
  Potato salad with sausage, 90
  Spanish potatoes, 94
  Stuffed peppers, 34
  Swiss cheese salad, 95

Tabbouleh with Fennel &
    Pomegranate, 87
Salmon, Mexican barbecued, 38
Sardines, with herb salsa, 42
Sausages, char-grilled, 21
Savarin with summer fruit, 114
Scallops with fennel & lime, 44
Scones, cheese & chive, 84
Shellfish, 11
Soups, 71
Squash, baked with Parmesan, 55
Squid, barbecued stuffed, 41
Strawberry croissants, 64
Sweet potato roulade, 103
Swiss cheese salad, 95

Tabbouleh, 87
Tea bread, dried fruit, 117
Tex-Mex burgers, 16
Thai spiced fish, 43
Tomatoes: sun-dried tomato
    bread, 82
Tortilla, potato & onion, 81
Tuna, char-grilled, 37
Turkey, stuffed, 100
  turkey rolls, 31

Vegetables, 11
  crudités, 70
  grilled Mediterranean, 52